ART

FOR YOUNG

AMERICA

MARGARET M. LEE
Art Supervisor, Division of Education
Carnegie Institute

MABEL B. TRILLING
Formerly Professor, Home Economics Education
Carnegie Institute of Technology

CHAS. A. BENNETT Co. Inc. PEORIA, ILLINOIS

Art for Young America

EDITOR'S INTRODUCTION

A *CONSISTENT,* youthful point of view has made ART FOR YOUNG AMERICA a textbook without counterpart in art education. Now, more than ever, it is dedicated to the world of early adolescence.

The new edition retains its analysis of historical high points; broadens the area in the recognition of beauty in nature and in man-made art. It re-explores the use of color; re-examines contemporary art influences in the entire life program. The writing style and choice of illustrations owe much of their appeal to a team of authors that includes a uniquely successful young teacher-artist.

Today, art is a functional and a practical part of the complex life which surrounds us. The men of business, industry, and commerce, the engineers, industrial designers, the city planners, the homemakers, and men and women in all walks of life now look to art as a significant phase of all their activities. Streamlined cars, airplanes, modern buildings of all kinds, bridges, parks, household furnishings, tools and equipment, books, magazines, newspapers, clothing, yards, even gardens—all are being transformed through art as much as through science to meet continually rising standards of living.

In this book the authors have skillfully outlined a broad course in art which meets the demands of the present day. It combines three major phases of the subject into one unified study, providing for creative activity, appreciational experiences, and for functional use of art knowledge.

THE EDITOR

PREFACE

*T*HE *THIRD EDITION* of ART FOR YOUNG AMERICA is based on the same philosophy of art education as that which inspired the original effort to provide simple and enjoyable art experiences for young people. It is designed for use by all students, talented or not, so that they may enjoy art in the world about them. Accordingly, emphasis is placed upon *appreciative experiences*. However, many suggestions for creative art activities are included so that the teacher may plan her course as best suits the needs and abilities of her pupils.

Believing that art in its many forms of expression is important to all people, the authors have endeavored to select subject matter which will appeal especially to the younger teen-age group. Materials for study cover a wide scope, ranging from the familiar things of everyday life to the great masterpieces of past historic eras. No attempt has been made to organize these subjects in terms of historical sequence. We leave that to a later time when students may become more interested in history of art.

Beginning high school students are ready and eager to explore the beauty of the world as they encounter it in nature and in various forms of man-made art. They are also interested in finding out what it is that makes some things more beautiful than others. This leads easily into a study of art principles, but only nominal attention is given to these well-known rules which often dominate the art course of study.

For students at the early adolescent period, it is important that they begin to discover beauty in their own environment, and to think about it in terms of pleasurable experience in living. The boy who sees a modern jet-propelled plane take off for its trip across the country is thrilled at the sight. His compelling interest in this giant of the airways makes him willing and ready to think about the modern airplane as a thing of beauty. Comparison of old and modern planes as presented in Chapter 2 helps him to find out why the recent models are more beautiful, and more or less consciously he begins to think in terms of art quality.

The chief objective in this book is to guide young people toward art as a way of life—to recognize beauty wherever it may be and to develop high standards of good taste. This can be accomplished only by keeping their art experiences on a pleasurable basis. Genuine appreciation cannot be imposed or "learned" like the multiplication table. We cannot induce the beauty experience by telling students that they *should* feel pleasurable responses. Psychologists tell us that the esthetic experience is due to a responsive attitude of mind in which the *pleasure tone is dominant.* Obviously we must pursue other methods of procedure than those which are successful in such subjects as mathematics or science. To insist upon our students liking the "best art" is futile and may easily result in a type of pseudo-appreciation which is unfortunate. Needless to say, no student should be made to feel inferior if he does not make the right choices. Whatever feeling we have for art, let it be genuine.

C. J. H.   M. M. L.

F. W. N.   M. B. T.

CONTENTS

1

ART IS FOR EVERYONE—ESPECIALLY YOU!

(Following page 16)

Do YOU LIKE the picture shown on the opposite page? You can scarcely help it, although you do not know what this strange-looking machine may be. The lovely, gay colors and the lively shapes capture your attention; you find that this unusual apparatus is pleasant to behold. Your reaction to the picture is an art experience in the enjoyment of beauty—an experience in art appreciation.

The mechanical device pictured here is known as the Solar Toy. It serves no useful purpose except to amuse and entertain. When the sun comes up, the toy begins to spin, dip, whirl, and curve in a symphonic circus of breath-taking color and dazzling motion. It is powered only by solar energy. At the touch of a sunbeam, the lightweight aluminum parts glide into their dizzy, swirling dance. Motors turn, wheels revolve, pistons rise and fall, and all the hues of the rainbow flash in the sunlight. At sundown, all movement and sound cease, for it operates only by the light of the sun.

Charles Eames, famous designer and architect, was commissioned by Aluminum Company of America to create this *abstract design* as part of Alcoa's Forecast program which explores new uses of aluminum for "the wonderful world of tomorrow."

The Enjoyment of Beauty

Inside each of us there is a hunger for beauty in our lives. Whether we realize it or not, each of us wishes for beautiful sights upon which to "feast our eyes." Psychologists tell us that we are born with this desire, so it is quite natural for each of us to seek beauty.

When we encounter something as delightful as the Solar Toy, we respond at once with an inner glow of pleasure. There are many things in the world that can arouse this warm, excited feeling—a flaming sunset; a golden palomino horse, with silver mounted bridle and saddle, prancing in a parade; a streamlined plane flashing across the sky; or a church spire reaching to heaven.

Enjoyment of beauty does not always depend upon such dramatic sights as those mentioned above. There are many features of everyday life that contribute beauty, though you may not notice some of them until you begin your study here. The lustrous surface of an aluminum pan and its pleasing contours may catch your attention in the kitchen. You may discover that the upholstery fabric on a living room chair looks very handsome against the color of the wall. Outside the house you may see the lacy pattern of budding tree branches against the sky, or pink and white petunias nodding in the sun. All day long you may see small displays of beauty at home, at school, and all around town— that is, if you have the eyes to see, and the inclination to enjoy them. Sometimes people seem to have a habit of mind which causes them to notice chiefly the things they *do not like,* and to express their feelings freely! This certainly does not endear you to your friends; most important of all, such a super-critical way of thinking prevents you from enjoying many worth-while things. Instead of saying, "I hate that color," or, "I can't stand that picture," it is better to look carefully at colors and forms and try to se-

lect the ones that you do like.   It may be that you will sometime
learn to like all colors, and many new forms, although you will always have favorites.

Nature Provides for the Enjoyment of Beauty

Everyone likes the tremendous bursts of beauty that nature puts
on display—a flaming sunset with marvelous colors streaming
across the sky, the tremendous snow-capped Rockies, the unbe-
lievably brilliant color of autumn leaves in the Adirondacks, a
far-reaching field of bluebonnets in Texas, a road through the
pine forests of Gifford Pinchot National Park in Washington,
the Grand Canyon in Arizona.   People take long trips to see such
sights as these and come home with undying memories of what
they have seen.   These experiences help to satisfy the need within
all of us to enjoy beauty.

Many people cannot take long trips across the country to see
certain spectacular sights, but they need not lack for beauty in
their lives.   Every locality has streets, parks, and other beauty
spots.   A single leaf can be beautiful.   The variegated coloring of
a begonia or a caladium may give you pleasure.   A small garden,
with bright old-fashioned flowers, is a lovely sight; even the
vegetable garden may contain attractive plants—for example, a
head of cabbage with its curly, cup-shaped leaves.

On page 88B you will find a picture of great charm, a color
photograph of Concord grapes on the vine.   Our study of color in
Chapter Five will help you to understand why this combination
of colors is so pleasing, but you can enjoy it now without any
explanation.

The study of beauty in animal forms is a fascinating subject.
It is fun to compare the lines and contours of different breeds of
dogs and to think of words which describe them.   For instance,

what dogs do you know that have long, flowing lines and slender proportions; short, well-rounded curves and almost square proportions; strong, forceful curves and powerful proportions?

It is interesting to see shapes and lines in the feline family—the lion, tiger, panther and your domestic cat. This kind of study will help you to observe more closely and to discover beauty where you had never before noticed it.

Art Quality in Many Kinds of Man-made Products

Our twentieth-century world is filled with thousands of small machine-made articles that were unknown a century or so ago, and here too we can find beauty. Designers spend much time and thought on eye-appeal so as to please prospective buyers. The same thing is true of automatic refrigerators and other large appliances. No one would wish to buy a household appliance only for its looks. Industrial engineers must be sure that the mechanical design of household appliances results in efficient operation. Functional efficiency and art quality are just as important when selecting household appliances or furnishings as when buying a house or an automobile.

Suppose that you are buying a new chair for the living room. Naturally, you want it to have good lines and be upholstered in a fabric which will harmonize with the other colors in the room. These things you can test with your eye, but what about functional quality? It is important to know whether it will be comfortable to sit in, yet many people buy chairs and davenports without trying them out for comfort. Other functional qualities include the effort required to move a chair about the room, and the cleaning ease of a fabric. A chair which requires two people to move it out from the wall on cleaning day, or one with fabric which does not clean well, can become a nuisance.

Think well about the functional nature of any article which you expect to be useful as well as beautiful. For example, what would you want in the design of a car besides good lines and color? Think of the head room, comfort of the seats, and other points. Remember that art and function are both important in a good car.

Enjoyment of Sculpture, Painting, and Architecture

So far we have been discussing art as it occurs in nature and the articles of everyday life, but we must include great art works of the past and present. A lifetime can be spent in the study of any one form of great art expression. However, you can get acquainted with examples of fine paintings, sculpture, and famous buildings. In later chapters you will find pictures and information which will help you to understand and enjoy these works of art. In your future travels you may some day see the originals of the paintings in art galleries. Some of the sculptures are also in art galleries, but many are located in parks and memorial plots. Famous buildings must remain in the sites where they were built.

Your interest and appreciation will be increased when you learn how and why some of them were created.

Do You Want Art in Your Home?

To some people this question may mean pictures on the walls and statues on the mantelpiece. These people mistake the real meaning of the question. A home may possess many art qualities and not have a single picture or statue in it.

Art in our homes means attractive outside appearance and surroundings; rooms that are convenient and inviting; the best wall, window, and entrance planning; furniture that is serviceable

Solar Toy.   BY CHARLES EAMES, FOR THE FORECAST COLLECTION OF ALUMINUM COMPANY OF AMERICA

and well proportioned; effective lighting, rugs, draperies, and upholstery that please us; lovely china, silver, and linens; in fact, good taste and visual pleasure in every detail.   Then we must arrange everything pleasingly—furniture, curtains, "traffic" lanes, ornaments, and utensils.   Isn't this a real challenge to all of us?

Everyone desires an attractive home.   It requires study.   We have to learn about colors, backgrounds, lines, and proportion. We use what we learn so that we may enjoy our homes more by investing in appearance wisely.   It requires definite planning, and an art course helps us now and in the future.

You can make your own room at home more interesting, more youthful.   A certain brother and sister who planned and finished a recreation room in the attic of their home made a big success of it because they had learned about color and design at school. The room is gay with blue and orange painted furniture, cretonne, rag rugs, and a large game box.   All their friends admire the room, and enjoy using it because it reflects their own young spirit.

Art Is for You

Anyone with eyes to see can find pleasure in the beauty of nature and in the art of man.   Experiences in art appreciation are really a search for beauty and you should think of it in terms of personal enrichment.   Do not be disturbed if you seem to lack talent in drawing and painting.   Enjoying art quality does not depend upon "special" ability.

Your study of this book should help you to attain high standards of good taste in various aspects of daily living—especially in such matters as selecting a home and home furnishing, flower arrangements, table settings, planning and planting a garden, and in personal dress.   You might become an unusually good artist in one of these activities.   Art is for everyone—especially you!

2

AUTOMOBILES, AIRPLANES, AND ART

H*AVE YOU EVER* seen a car that was built fifty years ago? That would be a very old car, yet automobiles were built even before that. The first ones looked more like carriages or buggies than self-powered machines, which is what the word "automobile" means. Look at the three cars on the next page. Figure 1. The uppermost model was built in 1908. The center one is a 1914 model; the lower one a popular 1931 model. The difference in appearance shows how much automobile design changed in just twenty-three years. You can see how the body style changed from a buggy style to a newer form. Now look at the 1959 car. Figure 2. You feel that this car is more powerful, is designed for more speed, and is certainly more comfortable to ride in than any of the others.

When we compare the newer model with the older ones, we notice at once how much "better looking" it is. A very great change has taken place from the horseless carriage of 1908 to the automobile of today. There will be new automobile designs in the future, and they may change greatly from today's models, but our knowledge of automobile construction, combined with the desire to improve design, will never allow us to return to the old-fashioned surrey with the fringe on top!

FIGURE 1. *These three cars show the development in automobile design.*
(Above) A 1908 model resembles the horse-drawn carriage, but without
a top. (Below) A 1914 model with lower, longer proportions. (Bottom)
A 1931 model with more pleasing lines and proportions.

FIGURE 2. A 1959 automobile designed with long, sweeping lines suggesting smooth, swift movement.

Study the lines of the three old cars. Notice especially how the 1908 model is built up of individual, box-like sections. As the models change from 1908 to 1931, there's a blending of the body sections, so that now the car appears to be designed as a unit. Notice how high these cars sit above the ground. This is because the wheels are large, and the body doesn't drop down between them. Instead, it's perched upon the axles, with much space above them. Even though the 1931 auto is an improvement over the older models, all three still have several things in common: The fenders, lights, horn, even the spare tire, appear to be tacked on rather than designed as parts of the body.

Now examine the 1959 car. The entire body and all its attached parts are designed as a unit, with each part fitting smoothly to the next. In fact, we can't see where one section joins another. This is because the designers of the car thought of it as one piece, instead of several pieces put together, such as you see in the older models. Now compare the lines of the cars. In the old cars the curves are short and not well related to the other lines. The fenders were bolted to the outside of the body for a purely functional reason; that is, because they were necessary. Without these fenders the water and mud from the road would be thrown up by the tires. Our new car has fenders, too, just as the old ones did, but we no longer identify them this way. They are hidden wells under the outside edges of the body, permitting a beautiful, unbroken line from front to rear. Notice especially the line from the headlight to the tip of the rear fender, and also the single, clean decorative strip which leads the eye swiftly from front to rear. The lines of the fenders and running boards of the old models seem awkward by comparison.

A study of the windshield and roof of the new model shows how they blend with the shape and structure of the car, while the windshields of the old models are poorly related to the general shape.

The design of the later model flows in long, straight lines and fine curves from the front to the back. The shorter lines blend with these long lines, helping to create the impression of quiet, smooth speed combined with a feeling of elegance.

Rhythm a Principle of Art

Everyone knows what is meant by rhythm in music. There are waltz rhythms, march rhythms, and other kinds. As we listen to music we are carried along by a succession of sounds repeated in *rhythm*. When we look at a streamlined design our eyes are carried along by its lines. The eye travels back and forth on these lines, and in a good design the eye will find many repetitions of the same or similar curves. This is rhythm in art.

Streamlining in the later model was considered at first quite an innovation. But streamlines were new only to automobiles and other industrial designs, not to the world of nature. Among dogs, the greyhound and Russian wolfhound are the streamlined models. The lines in their slim bodies, in their long heads and tails, and in their slender legs make a beautiful, rhythmic harmony, a harmony of lines that suggests swift movement.

There are different kinds of rhythm in art just as there are in music. When we study modern automobile design, we become acquainted with the kind of rhythm that is called streamlined. Later we shall learn about other rhythmic effects in art.

Streamlined Rhythms Suggest Speed

Streamlined rhythms such as those found in the lines of the modern automobile, the greyhound, or the sea gull as we have just said, are long and flowing. The eye can move rapidly from front to back or from head to tail without interruption. Even when there is no real movement of the object, the impression is that of great speed. Certainly this kind of rhythmic line is well chosen for the design of the modern motor car. Even trucks are now streamlined. Airplanes, trains, and boats offer other examples of streamlines in modern industrial design. In all these cases speed is desirable, and flowing, rhythmic movement in the design helps to create the impression of rapid movement.

Good Proportions Help

It is not only rhythmic line that makes the modern automobile more beautiful than that of forty or fifty years ago. The modern car is also more beautiful because of its finer proportions. The diagrams, Figure 3, show you the general proportions of the 1931 car pictured in Figure 1 as compared with the 1959 model, Figure 2. The hood, body, and rear deck or trunk of the recent model fit into a single, long, low rectangle. The older model is shorter, taller, and is high off the ground.

Which do you like better? Most people prefer the newer car.

FIGURE 3.   A comparison between the 1931 and 1959 automobiles. The 1931 model, A, is short, tall, and is high off the ground.   The 1959 car, B, fits a long, low rectangle.   It has smooth, powerful lines.

There are several important reasons for this.   The longer, lower car gives an impression of power and speed.   It seems less likely to tip over, and more likely to hold the road.   We feel safer in a lower car, especially at higher speeds.

Beauty of automobile design depends to considerable extent upon pleasing proportions and well-planned relation of spaces. It is fun to look at automobiles and try to see them in terms of proportions.   Look for small divisions of spaces as well as the large ones.   Can you find forms that are large, yet were designed to be inconspicuous?   Notice the roof and windows of the 1959 model, Figure 2.   See how thin the roof and supporting members are, compared with the larger mass of the body.   The low weight center almost prevents turning over at safe speeds.   The designers intended the roof of this car to be as inconspicuous and as lightweight as they could make it.   To achieve this, glass areas were made large, and roof supports small and thin. Thus the long, low look is not disturbed, and the car has a cleaner, uncluttered appearance. Do you think it would look as well with heavy supports and window frames?

The importance of good proportions in design was known to the world long before the automobile was invented. Even the buggy was beautifully proportioned for its purpose. More than two thousand years ago, the ancient Greeks designed a building with such perfect proportions that architects say it is the most beautiful building ever built. In a later chapter you will learn more about this famous building.

> Collect pictures of automobiles. Select three which you think most beautiful. Make diagram drawings of these three automobiles, showing the important lines and the general proportions. Your diagrams may be done in the style of Figure 3.

Engineers Created Modern Automobile Design

We must give credit to the engineers for producing some of the greatest beauty in our modern industrial world. Some of these engineers are really artists, and are often called "industrial designers." Instead of using brush and paint, they use steel, glass, and other materials required in the modern automobile. This is an excellent example of how beauty and usefulness may be united. The modern car has been made more and more useful to man. At the same time it became more and more beautiful.

Of course, some modern automobiles are more beautiful than others. In some the curves are finer and the proportions are more pleasing. In some the decoration is good; in others it is overdone. As you learn more about good design, you will be able to see these differences and to appreciate the best automobile design. Which of the most recent models do you consider most beautiful?

Automobile of the Future

Automobile design of the future will differ from that of the present. Small imported cars have an effect, because of their size and fuel economy. In the future engineers will find ways to improve mechanical features of the automobile, as well as styling, for greater beauty.

Perhaps the streamlined car will one day seem old-fashioned. Automobile design of the future may have a new and different kind of beauty, and, of course, we shall all buy the latest models that we can afford.

We should learn to see and enjoy beauty whether it is dated 1939 or 1969. Automobile design gives us a chance to study changing styles in art. Watch for the automobile designs of the future and compare them with designs of the past.

Beauty in Modern Airplanes

There has been as much change in the design of airplanes since the first models as with automobiles. Compare the old "flying-machine" and the modern airplane in Figure 4. It is a startling contrast. The power and beauty of the modern plane are impressive. The clumsiness of the older machine causes us to wonder that it could stay in the air even for a few minutes. We have only to look at the design of this old plane to understand why pilots referred to their machines as "crates."

The great beauty of the modern airplane depends partly on its splendid rhythmic lines. Long, forceful curves sweep from the nose to the tail of the ship and from tip to tip of the wing-spread. These lovely, rhythmic lines are echoed in the rudder and elevators at the tail of the ship. The whole design is made up of lines that are strong and swift. They express the purpose and function of the plane in marvelous fashion.

COURTESY PAN AMERICAN WORLD AIRWAYS SYSTEM

PHOTOGRAPH FROM U. S. NATIONAL MUSEUM

FIGURE 4. Two airplane designs with a decided difference in lines and proportions. A. Recent-model jetliner with fine streamlines and proportions. B. Curtiss pusher airplane made in 1909. The design is characterized by clumsy proportions and awkward lines.

26

The beauty of the modern plane depends also upon fine proportions in design. The large mass of body contrasts pleasingly with the wingspread. The rudder and elevators create smaller masses which combine harmoniously with the larger masses. Altogether it is an interesting arrangement of shapes and spaces.

The design of the older airplane has neither rhythmic lines nor interesting proportions. It is awkward and ugly. Improvement in the appearance of airplanes has been brought about because engineers were interested chiefly in designing machines that could fly better. As mechanical features of airplanes were changed, their appearance changed too. As planes became more powerful, more speedy, and more reliable, they also became more beautiful.

Anyone who has visited an airport and watched a mighty transport plane swoop down from the sky to the landing field knows that it is an exciting and dramatic moment. These giant beauties of the sky are like great birds that come and go on scheduled flights. Their strange beauty adds tremendously to the thrill of watching them land and take off. Imagine for a moment how you would feel if instead of the great streamlined plane you expected, a cratelike affair such as the old Curtiss pusher airplane dropped from the skies!

Art and Machines

There is beauty in modern machinery. Some people feel that real beauty is found only in the hand-painted picture or the hand-made object. However, we have found true beauty in machine-made products, automobiles and airplanes. Indeed, they are machines in themselves. There is beauty in many machines and mechanized conveyances or devices. You may find it in a train or a telephone, a boat or kitchen mixer.

A summary of the points discussed in this chapter should help us to see beauty in modern automobiles, airplanes, and other machines.

1. Smooth, flowing lines and form add to the effect of speed and power.

2. Streamlined designs possess one kind of beauty that we enjoy.

3. Interesting proportions help to produce beauty of design in automobiles, airplanes, and other mechanized conveyances and devices.

4. Transition from one line to another and from one form to another adds to the beauty of the streamlined design.

5. The beauty of modern automobile and airplane design was the result of engineering requirements. In this case art and efficiency of performance are united.

6. Some automobile and airplane designs are more beautiful than others. We should learn to see and enjoy the most beautiful examples of line and proportion.

SUGGESTIONS FOR ACTIVITIES

There are two different types of activities which you will find at the end of each chapter in this book. For those who like to draw, there is the type of problem which requires drawing and designing. This kind of problem we shall call a *creative activity*. For those who do not always care to undertake technical problems, there is the kind of problem which requires little or no drawing and designing. This type of problem we shall call an *experience in appreciation*. Your teacher will help you to decide which type of problem it will be better for you to attempt. Perhaps you will wish to try some of each kind.

EXPERIENCES IN APPRECIATION

1. Collect pictures of automobiles. From these pictures choose three, one which shows the best rhythmic streamlines, one which shows medium-

good rhythmic lines, and one which shows poor line. Mount each picture and label it to explain your opinion of the lines in the design.

2. Collect examples of transition of line and form. For example, the way a branch grows from a tree trunk or the way a handle is joined to a teacup.

3. Report some instance of how you saw and enjoyed beauty because of your study of rhythmic lines; because of your study of good proportions.

4. Collect airplane pictures. Hold a class exhibition of the most beautiful airplane pictures you can secure. Be prepared to point out why each design is good (or bad).

5. Arrange an exhibition of model airplanes made by the boys and girls in your school. If any of them are made to fly, arrange a test flight. Discuss the design points of each model.

CREATIVE ACTIVITIES

1. An imaginative problem: Design the airplane of tomorrow. Remember what you have learned about streamlines and good proportions.

2. Design the automobile of tomorrow.

3. Make a drawing of a streamlined train or boat.

4. Make a drawing of a streamlined automobile, top view. Some automobiles are very beautiful when seen from an upper window of a building. Some of the designs suggest giant beetles.

5. Try some imaginative drawings from new and unusual points of view. For example:

a. Think of yourself as a little field mouse crossing a super-highway. You look up and see a big, modern automobile speeding straight toward you, almost upon you!

b. Imagine that you are a seagull floating in the air high above the ocean. Suddenly you see a giant bird (an airplane) roaring across the sky just in front of you.

3

BEAUTY IN THE BEAST

W*HICH ANIMAL* do you think most beautiful? Possibly this question may be difficult for you to answer because you are not in the habit of looking for beauty in animal forms. In answering it, many people think first of the animal which they like best. If the horse is your favorite, you may say that the horse is the most beautiful. If you are a lover of cats you may say that the cat is the most beautiful. Either choice is good, provided you are thinking of the beauty of the animal and not of the lovable qualities that makes it your favorite pet.

In this chapter we are going to think of animals in terms of art study. You will find it interesting to think of animals in the same way that you did with cars and airplanes.

> Write down the names of two animals which you think are beautiful. Also write your reasons for these selections. Keep the paper until you have finished the study of this chapter.

Why Are Some Animals More Beautiful Than Others?

Good design in automobiles and airplanes depends to a large extent upon rhythmic lines and fine proportions. These qualities are also very important to beauty in animal forms. Automobiles and airplanes are designed by man and animal forms are designed by nature. Occasionally both designers make mistakes; lines are ugly and proportions awkward. At other times both these designers do fine jobs; lines are graceful and proportions pleasing. It is fun to study animal forms for these qualities, and to discover for ourselves the very fine designs that nature has created. There are other qualities besides rhythm and proportion which are important to beauty in an animal. Color and texture of the fur and hair covering the body of the animal may help to make it beautiful. Movement is another quality which contributes much to the beauty of an animal. Some animals are graceful, others clumsy and awkward. In the meantime look for animal pictures which you can cut from magazines and bring to class.

Beauty in the Dog Family

The dogs shown on the next page are purebred German shepherds. Often called "police dogs," of course this is the wrong name unless they are used for police work. Rin Tin Tin, who has appeared in motion picture and television stories, is a German shepherd.

German shepherds, famous for their intelligence and feats of courage, are strikingly handsome. The color picture on page 32B shows a dog standing naturally as he waits for the next command. Note the long, beautiful line from the tip of his ears, down over his back, and on to the tip of his tail, which is almost hidden by the hind leg. With your eye, trace the line from the tip of his nose, under the neck, under the body, and down the hind leg to the ground. As you study the conformation of the dog, you will see other rhythmic lines which blend together to make a pleasing effect. Notice also the proportions of the animal—strong neck and heavy shoulders, pointed ears, sturdy legs, strong jaws, expressing strength, alertness, and endurance.

The light and dark coloring of these dogs creates an interesting pattern against the middle gray background. If the dogs had been middle gray like the background, they would not have shown up well in the picture. When you take snapshots with your own camera, always think about the background, and plan so that your subject will stand out clearly.

At a dog show you will see many different breeds—each with its own particular style of beauty. This German shepherd posed for his picture just after he left the show ring, where he was judged "best of breed." For discussion of beauty in animals, see the chapter, "Beauty in the Beast."

There are dozens of kinds and breeds of dogs, and they come in many shapes and sizes—tiny, huge, shaggy, smooth coated, long legged, short legged, pointed eared, droop eared, and with all sorts of tails. In this variety of "designs" there are several types which you may prefer. Does it seem strange to you to think of a dog in terms of design and art quality? You will find it interesting, and need not let it interfere with your affection for any dog. This chapter is meant to help you see and enjoy beauty in animal forms. For example, you can derive a moment's pleasure at the sight of a handsome boxer dog strutting down the street, but this need not affect the warm, happy feeling that you have when your own dog comes to meet you as you return home. It is not necessary to *own* beauty in order to enjoy it. Love and admiration can be two different things.

> Start a collection of dog pictures. Every member of the class may bring as many as possible. Arrange the pictures on a bulletin board and discuss the different types of lines and proportions. Look for long, streamlined effects and slender proportions, for rounded curves and heavy proportions, and for other effects. Try to find "dog designs" which express dignity and nobility, graceful movement, strength and courage, fun and mischief, and other ideas.

The canine family includes certain wild animals, as well as dogs—the fox, wolf, and jackal. The fox is considered a rare beauty. He is small, graceful, and has a magnificent fur coat and tail, or brush. The fox has a reputation for being quick and cunning; hence there are many stories telling how he has escaped from the hunters on his trail. His beauty and personality are well expressed in the painting below. The Japanese artist, Mori Ippo, used a minimum of brush strokes to create the princely, graceful effect. The lines of the grasses echo the exquisite curves of body and tail. The sly, scheming character we attribute to the animal is emphasized in the drawing of the head. If you visit Boston, you can see the original of this painting, "The White Fox," in the Museum of Fine Arts of Boston.

FIGURE 7. *"The White Fox," by Mori Ippo, a Japanese artist of the nineteenth century.*

COURTESY, MUSEUM OF FINE ARTS, BOSTON

FIGURE 8. *Bronze panther by Guiseppe Moretti. Four of these statues are mounted at the corners of a bridge crossing Panther Hollow in Schenley Park, Pittsburgh, Pennsylvania.*

The Cat Family

Lions, tigers, panthers, and our own pet cats belong to a family that is famous for its smooth graceful beauty and its swift movement. "Quick as a cat" is an old saying. In the panther form shown above, you can see the lovely rippling rhythms of his strong muscles. It is easy to imagine the hair-trigger muscles sliding under his skin as he leaps through space.

The tiger has the same long, graceful lines as the panther, though his body is heavier in its proportions. It is easy to see that he belongs to the feline family. Anyone watching a tiger pace back and forth in his cage must be impressed both by his restless grace and power.

Our own pet pussy cats resemble the tiger even though many are marked differently. Indeed, they have been called "the tiger in the house."

35

A Very Old Cat from Egypt

The cat on the opposite page seems to have a waiting air. Perhaps she is still expecting to be returned to her home in Egypt where she was honored and well cared for some 2000 years ago. This statue was created to personify the Goddess Bastet, also called Bast, although the Egyptians did not worship cats or other animals. Sometimes they depicted them in animal form. The sculptor managed to give this cat statuette an air of serenity and nobility which they believed that a goddess would have.

Note the ear rings adorning Bastet. Perhaps you can see traces of the necklace which they put around her neck. The surfaces of the statue are mottled and pitted now, but probably were once smooth and glossy.

Cats were held in respect by the Egyptians to such an extent that they mummified dead pets, and when a house cat died, members of the household would go into mourning for it. Egyptians felt that cats were of great service to them, as indeed they were. Stored cereal grains, the main food for the people, were often infested by hordes of mice and rats. Only the cats could save their grain from destruction, and for this protection the Egyptians were most grateful. The penalty for killing a cat was death. Cats are still the most effective means of controlling rodents.

If you are fond of cats, you may be interested in learning more about them and their different characteristics. You might consult the encyclopedia and books about cats for information about Persian and Angora cats—the long-haired beauties; the Siamese cats, which are considered the aristocrats of the short hairs; the Manx cat, which is born with only a stub tail; and the tortoise shell, which got its name because of its mottled coat.

You will find it interesting to collect pictures of cats—especially kittens.

"Citation in the Home Stretch"—Lithograph by *C. W. Anderson.*

Horses Come in Different Styles

It is just as much fun to study lines and proportions in horses as in cats and dogs, even more fun if you happen to like horses better. There is considerable variation of lines and contours in the horse (equine) family. Types range from race horses to Shetland ponies and from zebras to army mules. The race horse in full action is a splendid example of concerted rhythmic movement. It is worth a trip to the race track to see and hear the magnificent fleet-lined animals thunder past on their way to the finish line.

38

The race horse on the opposite page is Citation putting on a burst of speed as he comes down the home stretch to win. The artist, C. W. Anderson, knows horses very well. Dating from his early days on the plains of Nebraska, he has studied horses and their characteristics. In the following paragraph, he tells you in his own words why he chose to depict Citation coming down the home stretch.

"I have always been a great admirer of Citation, considering him to be our greatest horse since Man O' War. He had unusual beauty and was perfection itself in action. His stride was so smooth and rhythmic that he seemed to flow over the ground. In this lithograph I chose that split second before he is off the ground with all four feet because the sweep of line of the near fore leg is carried through the shoulder and neck to the tip of the ears in a driving tangent that to me gives the feeling I had in watching him cut loose with the surging drive that smothered his opposition."

The artist has made us feel the power and drive of the running horse with his skillful drawing. The jockey, standing in his stirrups, crouches low over Citation's neck. He almost seems to be part of the horse. The feeling of speed is accentuated by the flying mane and tail, and by the clouds of dust where Citation's hoofs have dug into the dirt track. Most important, in creating the feeling of swift movement, is the line mentioned by the artist in the paragraph above. The line of the right front leg, up over the neck to the tip of the ears, expresses the dynamic quality of the horse's action.

You will notice that the artist omitted any suggestion of the race track in the background. If he added any items such as the bleachers filled with excited, screaming people, or even the rails alongside the track, they would have distracted our attention from the speed motif of the horse.

"The Jockey" by Hunt Diedrich.

Present-day sculptors have used the horse form to create many splendid effects. Instead of realistic forms, they sometimes make what might be called "design horses." The race horse above is certainly not a *real* looking animal and neither is the jockey realistic. This a rather playful interpretation of a jockey on his thoroughbred prancing to the starting post. Slender proportions are exaggerated, some of the surfaces are flattened, and the whole effect is delightful. Such details as the jockey's face, the stirrups, the bridle, and the reins have been omitted. This serves to center our attention upon the spirited horse, who is eager to be off.

"St. Martin" by Sidney Waugh is an interesting interpretation of a horse and rider which is very different from "The Jockey" on the opposite page.

The great horse in the picture above is in striking contrast to the prancing steed on the opposite page. His huge body is emphasized by curves which make you think of the power of his bulging muscles. You may have seen this type of horse at a county fair where Percherons and Belgians have been exhibited. They are called draft horses because they are bred to pull heavy loads. Draft horses have been almost entirely replaced in our country by trucks and heavy machinery, but when we see them in the show ring or as a matched six-horse team in a parade, the effect is one of powerful, dramatic beauty.

The war chargers ridden by the knights of the Middle Ages were strong, heavy horses which could bear the weight of the steel armor worn by their riders. It is said that the knights sometimes wore armor so heavy that they could not climb onto their horses without assistance.

The jockey and his horse make us feel the excitement of the horse and his eagerness to break into action. But in the case of the war charger, there is little effect of movement. The charger stands with all four feet planted firmly on the ground and the rider sits easily in the saddle. The sword points downward while St. Martin holds up his coat as though he were about to hand it to someone on the ground.

St. Martin lived in the fourth century, a very long time ago. One of the things for which he was remembered was the gift of his coat to a beggar. This is the incident in the life of St. Martin which the sculptor chose to portray.

St. Martin was born a heathen in Pannonia, an ancient country of central Europe. As a young soldier he was converted to Christianity and eventually became the bishop of Tours, France. He is famous for his stand against drunkenness and because he tried to prevent the slaughter of the Priscillianist heretics.

His coat became a venerated possession of the Frankish kings, who carried it about in a portable shrine. His feast, Martinmass, is November 11th. In England, the warm, balmy weather about that time of the year, which corresponds to our Indian summer, is called St. Martin's summer.

After reading this story about St. Martin, look again at his picture on page 43. The statue should now have a new meaning

"Moonlight Madness."

to you, and you can see how the sculptor symbolized the life of St. Martin in a modern work of art.

Horses are a popular subject with painters as well as with sculptors. An American artist, Phil Paradise, who painted the picture shown above, calls it "Moonlight Madness." The horses are stirring about in the pasture back of the barn, excited and playful in the light of the moon. It seems as though the forms are really moving as you look at the picture. You can almost hear the hoofs on the ground, the squeals and whinnies. In this picture the moon-lit horse forms are the center of interest. They are more important than the tree, barn, farmhouse, or sky. Everything is subordinated to the animal movement. Remember this, because later on we shall study a principle of art which is called emphasis.

Art and Animals

It is a good idea to round up our ideas occasionally and find out what we have learned. Here are some points to remember from our study of beauty in animals.

1. Some animals are more beautiful and interesting in their appearance than others, and it is fun to compare them. Discrimination will help us to see and enjoy beauty in the animal world.

2. "Good lines" are very important to beauty in animal forms. In art we call it rhythm.

3. Fine proportions are characteristic of beautifully built animals. Exaggerated proportions disturb our sense of beauty.

4. A balanced effect is important. Too much weight in one portion of the body upsets our sense of equilibrium.

5. Contrasts of light and dark and color make some animals more interesting in appearance.

6. The texture of the animal's fur may contribute greatly to his beauty. For example, compare the fur of a fox with the hide of an elephant.

7. Movement is an important factor in the beauty of an animal. Some animals move with smooth, gliding action, others with a jerky waddle.

$\longrightarrow$

"Job's War Horse," a lithograph by George Ford Morris, has great dramatic appeal. The artist says, "There are few Bible students who are not familiar with the stirring description of the horse in war, in the book of Job, which I took in this instance for inspiration.

" 'Hast thou given the horse strength: hast thou clothed his neck in thunder? . . . The glory of his nostrils is terrible. . . . He mocketh at fear and is not affrighted; neither turneth he back from the sword!' " (Job 39:19–25.)

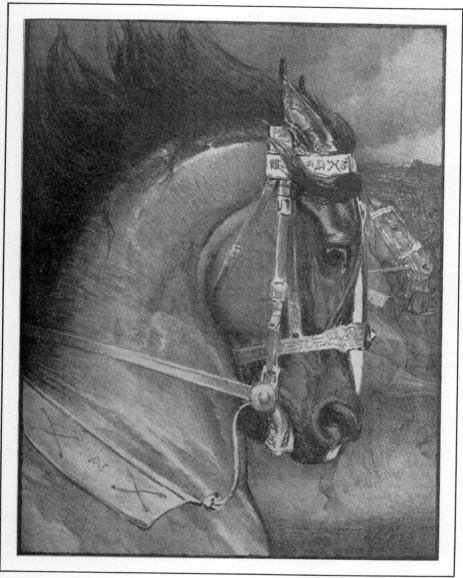

EXPERIENCES IN APPRECIATION

1. Select an animal family for study of lines and proportions. You might take the dog family, including the wolf, fox, and coyote, or the rodents, including the rabbit, squirrel, and woodchuck. Make a series of diagrams showing characteristic lines in each member of the family.

2. Start a scrapbook of animal pictures. Organize the pages of your book to show animals which have particularly pleasing rhythmic line, fine proportions, lovely textures, those built for swift action, and those revealing great strength.

3. Observe animals at the circus, in the zoo, and on the farm. Watch their movements. Write three "word pictures" describing their characteristic movements.

4. Study the work of the great animal painter, Rosa Bonheur. Collect copies of her paintings and report to the class what you have learned about her work and her life.

5. Study the work of Frederic Remington, the American artist who painted the "Wild West." If possible, secure one of the books which he illustrated and show it to your classmates.

6. Arrange a day for an exhibition of small animal statues. Bring to class any small animal figures which you can secure. These may include wood carvings, pottery, soap carvings, or glass animals. Discuss these little animal figures for the points listed on page 46.

CREATIVE ACTIVITIES

1. Choose an animal family and make a series of sketches showing characteristics of different members of the family. Work from live animals where possible.

2. Choose one animal with which you are familiar. Make sketches of different views; side, front, three-quarters, and back.

3. Choose an animal which you think has a particularly beautiful texture in its fur covering. Using crayons or colored pencils make a sketch trying to show the quality of the texture.

4. Choose an animal which you think has a decidedly individual, characteristic style of movement. Draw it in action. Is it smooth and fast, slow and easy, quick and jerky, or clumsy? Experiment with different kinds of lines to see which ones will best express the characteristic action.

5. Hold an exhibition of the animal drawings made by the class. Select a judge to choose the three which he likes best and to tell you his reasons.

4

TREES, CLOUDS, WIND, AND WATER

S*OME PEOPLE* think that trees are beautiful only when they are dressed in all their foliage. Perhaps these people value trees only as shade from the sun. Other people know that trees may be very beautiful when bare of all leaves. Indeed, bare tree branches may even seem more beautiful than when covered with foliage. Why? Because some bare tree branches make such beautiful patterns against the sky that it seems almost a pity to hide them with leaves. Of course, if you think of tree branches only as a support for leaves in summertime you will not understand this, but with a little study, you see their beauty.

Patterns in Tree Branches

There are as many different patterns in tree branches as there are trees in the world. It is this endless variety which adds so much interest to the study of tree patterns. However, trees of the same species show the same characteristic lines of growth in their branches, although each individual tree differs from all other trees. We'll look at some types of tree branchings that you might see in your own backyard or along the street. These are common trees, the kind that grow in many parts of the country. Look first at the

47

FIGURE 17, left

Locust trees in winter. An irregular pattern with staccato movement.

FIGURE 18, below left

A maple tree with radiating branches, full and round.

FIGURE 19, below right

An elm tree with fanlike spread, tall and stately.

FIGURE 20. Two elms in front of an old house in Salem, Massachusetts.

pattern of the locust, page 50. You will see at once that it is entirely different from other kinds of trees. It is irregular, with sudden little turns at unexpected places—a staccato movement. There is surprise in every branch.

The two trees in Figures 18 and 19 are the elm and the maple. At first glance, the line of growth may seem similar in the two trees. But then you see the branches of the maple in the first picture spread out fanlike and curve skyward. They form a symmetrical pattern, round and full like the top half of a circle. The lower branches grow straight out from the trunk, which makes the maple an excellent shade tree. The branches of the elm also spread out fanlike, but they grow nearly straight up, then begin to curve gradually outward. Some of the heavy outer branches curve earthward in a graceful arc. The elm grows tall and stately, and lends dignity to fine homes and lawns.

The two giant elms in Figure 20 make a beautifully balanced, symmetrical arrangement. They are very old trees and perhaps

49

FIGURE 21. A painting by Lauren Ford called "No More Room at the Inn." Part of its charm is due to the tree patterns against snow and sky.

not so graceful as the younger elms, but their trunks and branches are strong and sturdy. They impress us with their gracious dignity. Be sure to notice the lovely shadow tracery on the front of the old house. Often shadows cast by tree branches on a wall or across a window furnish us with delightful bits of beauty.

Artists have discovered the beauty of trees in winter, and sometimes paint the loveliness of bare tree branches against the snow and sky. The painting called "No More Room at the Inn" by Lauren Ford, an American woman, is a charming scene, Figure 21. The picture is full of human interest. We like the children, the horses, the barns, and the old house. But think how deserted the place would seem without the trees. They make a strange, fascinating pattern against the snow and sky.

Still another pattern is found in the fruit trees that bloom in the spring. The painting called "A Pear Tree" by Edward Bruce, Figure 22, is a lovely interpretation of delicate, white pear blossoms against a blue sky.

A Closeup Look

How often have you stopped to look at a tree closely? The bark of a tree is beautiful, too, and very interesting. A look at Figure 23 will show you how trees differ in bark patterns.

FIGURE 22. "A Pear Tree," by Edward Bruce.

COURTESY, DR. JAMES B. MURPHY

The bark of ponderosa pines (A) is furrowed, giving the appearance of great strength and old age. These trees grow very tall, and are straight and strong. As they grow the bark splits open, renewing itself from inside. The top surface is rough and scaly, and flakes come off as the spring growth begins and the tree swells in size. This scaly surface makes a beautiful pattern of delicately shaded patches, bordered by strong, deep, vertical furrows.

Compare such rugged texture with the smoother quaking-aspen bark (B). Here the bark hugs the tree closely, like a thin, tight skin, and has no rough scales or grooves. A series of irregularly spaced horizontal lines or wrinkles in the bark climb ladder-like up the tree to be lost in the foliage. This bark differs from that of the pine in another way. It grows with the tree instead of cracking open as the tree grows. It shows the stretch of growth in the wrinkles formed around the branch stubs. Only at the base where the bark is very thick does it show any splitting. Can you name another tree that has a horizontal growth pattern in its bark? How about the cherry tree? Or the birch?

The third example, the hemlock (C), has a rough bark somewhat similar to the pine, but the scales are smaller and more evenly spaced. Although at first glance the hemlock appears to be less rugged than the pine, actually it is rougher. This tree has what is called a shaggy bark. The sections or scales turn out at the sides and bottom, giving them the appearance of very old shingles. And their purpose is the *same as shingles,* to protect the tree as shingles protect a house.

Try some "closeups" yourself. Compare the textures of the bark from several trees. Can you find interesting patterns such as shown in Figure 23? How do old trees differ from young ones? What trees in your neighborhood have the most interesting bark?

FIGURE 23. Bark Textures

A. *Ponderosa pine* (right)

Rugged and furrowed, showing
    great strength.

B. *Quaking aspen* (left, below)

A thin, tight skin-like bark with
    horizontal growth pattern.

C. *Hemlock* (right, below)

A shaggy bark, with "shingles" to
    protect the tree.

A

B   COURTESY, U. S. FOREST SERVICE   *C*

Trees in Summertime

Nearly everyone enjoys the sight of a fine tree in full leaf on a summer day. Such a tree may appeal to some people chiefly as a good shade tree; if it is a fruit tree some will think first of its delicious fruit; if it is a very large tree some will think of its beautiful wood. The people who have learned to get the most enjoyment out of trees will look at a splendid tree also for its beauty. They will note its shape. Is it tall and stately? Or low and spreading? Are the masses of foliage interesting in shape?

No matter in what part of the country you may live, you will find trees that are interesting and lovely. The four trees in Figure 24 grow in widely separated sections of the country. The great elm tree, A, stands in Durham, New Hampshire. Perhaps you have passed it on a motor trip. It is a magnificent sight with its great masses of foliage that sway gracefully in the breeze. There are many of these giant elm trees in the eastern and New England states, and everyone should learn to know them. The tree in Figure 24 B is a eucalyptus that stands in Fresno Country, California. It is as lovely and graceful as the elm tree in New York, but in its own characteristic way. Notice the great masses of delicate, lacy foliage. If you live in California you surely know these lovely trees. If you plan to visit the state, remember to look for the beautiful eucalyptus trees.

How many trees that grow in your locality can you recognize by their characteristic shapes? A study of the three trees shown on the next page will help you to become acquainted with trees in full leaf. The white elm (A) is a graceful tree which has been compared to a vase of flowers. The eucalyptus grows differently, its masses of foliage creating a tall, domelike shape. The old oak tree has grown into a broad, spreading mass.

This enormous oak tree shown in Figure 24 C stands in the city

A

B

FIGURE 24. *Three beautiful trees from different sections of the country.*
A. An elm tree in Durham, New Hampshire. B. A eucalyptus tree in
Fresno County, California. C. Treaty Oak in Austin, Texas.

C

of Austin, Texas. Estimated to be over five hundred years old, it
is known as Treaty Oak because it is believed the first boundary-
line treaty with the Indians was made here. In those days the
branches could not have been so low. Notice the low and spreading shape of the tree. Its lower branches actually rest upon the
ground. The whole effect is that of great strength and age.

The search for beauty in trees with bare branches or in full
foliage is a fascinating hobby. There is beauty, too, in forests or
groves where trees grow close together. The forest scene on the
opposite page has a stirring, wonderful beauty. The great tree
trunks reaching to the skies create a lovely pattern of vertical lines,
and the sunlight filtering through from above makes a delightful
play of light and shadow. Notice the interesting texture of the
bark on the tree trunks in the foreground.

Following the straight sentinels of the forest are some trees
unique to the south. (Page 60.) These are live oaks from Louisiana. In this warm, moist climate, vegetation thrives more than
in dry climates. One can find things growing here that won't grow
in the north, or in the hot deserts. This is evidenced by the moss
hanging from the branches of the oaks. Looking up through these
trees, one feels he might be in an enchanted forest. How beautiful
this grove must be when the wind breathes through the moss, caus-
ing it to sway gently, creating moving, lace-like patterns. The
branches of the trees seem to be spreading gracefully to display
the moss growing upon them. Like all oaks, the branches twist
and turn in sturdy curves, as if they were sure of each movement.
It is this growth pattern that gives oaks the appearance of great

⟶

COURTESY, U. S. FOREST SERVICE

FIGURE 25, page 59. *Tall and straight Douglas Firs, Mt. Baker
National Forest, Washington*

Live Oaks in Louisiana, showing the lacy pattern of moss growing from the branches.

strength.   Like the Treaty Oak of Austin, Texas, these trees are very old, for their branches spread far out, and almost touch the ground in some places.   Anyone visiting Louisiana or other Gulf coast states may see trees draped with this beautiful lacy moss.

There are many other trees that have histories.   Some are famous landmarks, while others remain to remind us of the ways in which our country was settled.   One of the latter is the massive hackberry tree which was planted by the Rappites when they founded New Harmony, along the Wabash River in Indiana.

This tree is over 150 years old, is one of the largest of its kind in the United States. The trunk is 22 feet around, 100 feet high.

Massive hackberry tree at New Harmony, Indiana. Its strong curves and sturdy base suggest great strength.

The girls standing beside the tree show how immense it is. Its size and strongly curved branches suggest great strength. To look at the tree one might easily believe that it will last another 150 years. Its wide flaring trunk must lead from a very large root system. It seems as if it has reached out at the base to get a good grip on the earth in order to support its tremendous spread and weight.

Probably one of the most interesting trees of all is the banyan. Even the name sounds strange, doesn't it? Look at the picture at the bottom of the page. See how the branches grow out from the trunk, then reach down to the ground to support themselves as they wander off. They appear to be standing on many legs. What an interesting pattern of vertical lines and near-vertical angles they make. Of course, these trees can best be appreciated

Banyan Tree. Growing extra legs for support, these trees grow out and down as well as up.

COURTESY, RINGLING MUSEUMS, SARASOTA, FLORIDA

in color. Their rich, sun-warmed tans and grays make them stand out in subtle, beautiful contrast to the greens in the leaves and other vegetation. The sunlight filtering through from above adds a warm glow, producing a dappled pattern over the entire display. This giant banyan tree, growing on the grounds of the Ringling Museum of Art in Sarasota, Florida, is typical of some of the exotic tree forms to be found in this state.

Trees are nearly always more beautiful when we view them as part of a larger natural scene. At the beginning of the chapter we discussed several tree forms that we might find growing near our homes or some other place close by. The winter branches we saw seemed a bit out of place, because we saw them alone. Actually, trees are most beautiful when they become an integral part of a landscape, or as shade trees planted in a fine lawn or garden. On page 64 A are two photographs in color of trees in landscapes. The photos show the contrast between trees in winter and summer. The delicate, lacy black of the trees in the upper photograph are especially beautiful when viewed next to the simple, massive shape of the red barn and the blanket of snow. They provide the contrast that creates exciting variety in what might otherwise be an ordinary scene. Have you ever had an opportunity to see a beautiful winter landscape such as this?

The lower photograph displays the beauty of trees in summer, with their intricate and many-shaded leaf patterns. There is also a distant stand of lush, dark green foliage that provides a very handsome backdrop for the red farm buildings. Farmers take advantage of trees in many ways. They provide effective wind-breaks against winter's cold, and hold back the drifting snow. Trees near the house keep it cooler on hot days by providing shade.

State governments maintain forestry departments to protect their trees, for they realize that thoughtless or greedy people

A painting by Daniel Garber called "Old Tree, Chalfont."

might one day destroy the remaining forest lands of our country.

Artists have studied the beauty of form and pattern in trees since landscape painting was first attempted. An American painter named Daniel Garber is well known as a painter of trees. The magnificent old tree change is a fine subject for one of his paintings. Study the strong, graceful curves in the sturdy branches, the billowy masses of foliage, and the delightful play of light and shadow in the foliage and on the tree trunk. Notice especially the great branch hanging down almost to the ground. See how the weight of this mass is balanced on the other side by the long branch that swings upward and to the left.

The photograph on page 66 was taken early in the morning. The sun is low in the sky, so it throws long shadows on the ground, creating a beautiful effect. It isn't often we see scenes like this. The sun is at the level of the trees and shines through them, creating an almost luminous effect in the background. This effect is called backlighting. It's used by artists and photographers alike to produce unusual lights and shadows in their compositions.

Trees in the Wind

Trees are fascinating subjects for study to lovers of beauty at any season of the year. In winter there are the intricate patterns of bare branches, in spring the lacy loveliness of budding leaves, in summer the splendid glory of full foliage, and in autumn the exciting spectacle of gorgeous color. Sometimes it is the wind that turns designer, and gives our trees new forms. When the graceful branches of the elm tree sway gently in the breeze, we catch glimpses of rhythmic movement. When a stiffer breeze blows through young maples, we see more forceful line patterns as the trees bend with the wind.

Beautiful Effects in Water

Oceans, lakes, rivers, and brooklets take up so much space in our world it is fortunate that in them we find innumerable glimpses of beauty. These beautiful effects found in water vary greatly. The surface of a lake may act as a mirror. This happens only when the water is still and no wind ruffles its surface. When water tumbles over a waterfall and rushes along in a swift, boiling torrent the effect is very different. The first photograph on the opposite page is a good example of turbulent water. Frothy white lines with violently changing pattern help to make us feel the violence and power of the water's movement. It can be awe-inspiring.

An unusual pattern of trees and shadows. Effects like this are caused by backlighting, which means the light is behind the object.

The delicate, lacy black of the trees in the upper photograph is a beautiful contrast to the simple large mass of the red barn and the white blanket of snow. The lower photograph suggests the beauty of sunlit trees, as interesting foreground detail as well as a handsome backdrop for the farm buildings.

64A

Turbulent water with violently changing pattern.

Quieter effect of gently rippled surface.

Reflections in still water. Beauty in complete repose.

64B

A more gentle effect created by moving water is that shown in B, the center picture, page 64B. The tiny ripples in the surface make a quietly moving rhythmic pattern. One can imagine how the sunlight might dance from these wavelets, each of them a mirror to catch the bright, warm radiance.

When there is little or no wind to disturb the water's surface, reflections play an important part in producing beautiful effects. In the lower picture, C, page 64B, the water is slightly disturbed, blurring the reflection into delightful, strange, wavering shapes. These shapes are often more fun to watch than the sharp, clear reflections from a perfectly smooth surface.

Some effects on the water's surface come and go so quickly that the eye must be quick to catch their beauty. The camera's eye caught the fine effect shown on the next page. The canoe paddle produced the pattern of circles as it was lifted from the water. Notice how the reflection of the paddle adds interest to the composition.

Relate to the class a description of the most beautiful water effect that you have ever seen. Did the effect depend on rhythmic line patterns, effect of light and dark, or reflections for its beauty?

The ocean gives us certain effects that are not possible in smaller lakes or rivers. When the great ocean waves come rolling in and break against the rocky shore the effect is splendidly dramatic. The seascape, page 68, called "Meridian," was painted by Frederick J. Waugh, a famous American artist. He has made his picture interesting through the sharp contrasts of white water and dark rocks and through the effects of sunlight and shadow. Here we can feel the tremendous power of the sea as the great waves thunder in and crash against the rocks. This kind of painting is very realistic. The artist shows us the sea as it actually looks.

"Water Rings," a photograph by Ernest Schnizer, shows a beautiful pattern in water.

"Meridian," a painting by Frederick Waugh, shows the tremendous power of the sea.

In Mr. Waugh's painting we felt the excitement and strength of the sea. At the bottom of this page is a lithograph by Joe Jones, who sees the water in a very different way. We can be sure he found contentment in this scene, for with a sure, yet delicate line he has captured a peaceful mood. He must have chosen a clearing sky for a special reason. Don't you think he felt the freshness in the air just as you do after a storm? The men in the boat close to us in the picture seem to be preparing to hoist their sail. One feels that they'll get the sail up just as the clouds pass over. The day will be bright, and the breeze fresh and clean. These two photographs combine trees and water. You may have found beautiful scenes like these yourself during your summer vacation.

"Reaching for the Sun," a lithograph by Joe Jones, showing a peaceful mood with a sure, delicate line.

The upper photograph emphasizes the slender silhouettes of the trees; the lower one uses the water as its center of interest. Each is a good composition, having been carefully planned before the picture was taken. A complete range of values gives these scenes vitality.

Clouds Tell a Story

Clouds tell the story of the weather.   When we look at the sky and see huge masses of dense clouds above us, we say, "It's going to rain."   And near the end of the storm, when we see the blue of the sky showing through, we say, "The storm is over!"   What shapes of clouds do you see when you think of an approaching storm? Have you ever looked into the sky on a hot summer day, to see only a few white puffs that seem to hang there motionless?   Do you recall having looked up to see those wispy, silken threads stretched out for great distances high up in the sky?   Clouds like these often tell us of a change in the weather that may be a day or two away.

Some people enjoy looking at clouds to find the shapes of things they know.   Giant animals, great ocean liners, or even fleets of space ships take shape high in the sky.   Other folks just like to look at clouds because it makes them "feel good."   Haven't you felt a thrill in watching great cloud forms glide swiftly and silently across the sky?   Surely the softly tinted shapes in a fading sun-set give you a feeling of contentment and joy at just being alive as they lie there unmoving on the horizon, their arms stretching high to catch the last warm light of the setting sun.

The illustrations on the next page show how clouds can help to make a good picture.   Without clouds these two pictures wouldn't be nearly so interesting, nor would they have the feeling of great distance they appear to have now.   The first picture shows a cloud formation almost exactly like the one Joe Jones saw when he drew his harbor scene, "Reaching for the Sun."   See how the sun's rays are just beginning to burst through the thin edges of the clouds.   It looks as if the sun were actually pushing the clouds away, pointing beams of warm light at the glistening landscape below.   In both photographs lacy branches form a deli-cate border around the scenes.   They contrast sharply with the

A. The sun's rays burst through the thin edges of the clouds.

B. Lacy branches contrast with soft cloud masses.

cloud masses. Looking at the sky through the branches of trees can be a memorable experience. The branches become silhouettes of dark lace against a sky that seems brighter than usual. "Frame" some pictures like this for yourself.

Sometimes we overlook beauty in the "ordinary" things because we see them so often, and we're used to them. An American artist named John Rogers Cox shows us that an ordinary scene can be beautiful, and unusual! In his painting, "Wheat Shocks," Mr. Cox tells us a story about a farmer. One can almost believe he is standing with us, looking past the rotted old fence post toward his field of drying hay. The cloud standing motionless in the deep blue sky emphasizes the loneliness of the scene. Do you, too, feel the heat rising from the dry earth as the wheat shocks stretch in lonely vigil as far as the eye can see? How glad the farmer must be that his summer's work has been so successful.

"Wheat Shocks," a painting by John Rogers Cox.

COURTESY, LEON FALK, JR.

In the Japanese print shown in Figure 31, the artist has combined the elements mentioned in the title of this chapter—trees, clouds, wind, and water.   In this case the rain falls from the dark clouds and is driven across our vision at an angle by a strong wind.   Tree branches in the foreground bend and sway in the wind.   Farther away growing dimmer in the distance other tree branches bow their heads under the force of the wind and rain. Two pedestrians going down the hill protect themselves from the rain, one with an umbrella and the other with his big hat.   The others climb the hill at a slower pace.   The first one is shielded from the rain by his big hat and straw rain coat.   The other two are coolies who bear a litter which carries a passenger who is almost entirely covered with some kind of tarpaulin.

In this print the artist had no thought of realism, but rather was trying to create a lovely, decorative effect.   It is a lovely rhythmic pattern with delicate gradations of light and dark.   Strong rhyth-

FIGURE 31.   *A Japanese print called "Rain Storm at Shono Pass," by the famous artist Hiroshige.*

mic movement is created by lines suggesting the rain, by the swing to the left of the branches, the thatched roof tops, the figures which bend forward, and the line of the hill. These are combined in pleasant, harmonious pattern.

Have you ever noticed the special kind of beauty that hovers over the landscape on a rainy day? Trees, hills, and buildings seem to be painted in delicate tones of silvery grays. Ugliness is blotted out with a strange, mysterious beauty. On the next rainy day, look carefully, and perhaps you will see a magic transformation of some familiar scene.

Beauty Is Where You Find It

In our study of art so far we have found beauty both in nature and in things made by man. Animals and airplanes, trees and automobiles, often provide us with moments of special enjoyment if we can pick out rhythmic lines, proportions, and balanced arrangement, which help to produce beauty. Again and again we have seen how these factors produce pleasing effects. Rhythmic form is an old friend by this time. As we continue our study we shall see that it is important in many ways. This is also true of good proportions, balance, emphasis, and other art principles. To know how these principles are used both in nature and in man-made objects helps us to enjoy beauty wherever we find it.

EXPERIENCES IN APPRECIATION

1. Select a tree in your neighborhood which you think has beautiful, rhythmic movement in the branches. Make some line drawings that show the kind of curve and direction of growth. Your drawing need not be a picture of the tree, but merely a kind of diagram which shows that you can see the formation of the branches. Making these lines will help you to feel and enjoy their beauty.

2. Collect pictures of trees which you think are beautiful. Label each picture, explaining the chief claim to beauty.

3. Collect pictures of oceans, lakes, and streams. Try particularly to get different effects. Use pictures that include interesting or dramatic cloud formations. Label each picture to explain why the effect is beautiful.

4. Write a description of some effect in water that you have seen and thought beautiful. Trying to match words to what we see with our eyes often helps to increase our enjoyment of beauty.

5. If you have a camera try to get a good picture of the most beautiful tree which you can find. If several members of the class can do this, plan a day for an exhibition of tree snapshots by class members. Perhaps you will enjoy making a hobby of tree pictures. Try to get the same tree in all four seasons of the year and also when the wind is blowing.

CREATIVE ACTIVITIES

1. Make a series of "tree portraits." Select three trees of distinctly different types. Make pencil drawings showing characteristic growth and formation. Make a series of color sketches of the same trees, using water color, crayons, or soft chalk.

2. If you should make a hobby of tree pictures, you will find it interesting to make portraits of the same trees in different seasons and during different kinds of weather. The same tree in winter on a fine, sunny day, or during a snowstorm gives very different effects. The same tree on a windy day in spring or on a rainy day in November shows still different effects. Probably there will not be time for you to carry out all these projects as classwork, but they are good suggestions for fun outside of school if you like to draw and paint.

3. Plan a dramatic, story-telling picture with trees as the chief "actors." The success of your picture will depend on how well you imagine the effect that you wish to create. You might wish to create an effect that is strange, weird, and frightening. Or you might prefer to make a picture which expresses gaiety and lively happiness. There are many other effects which you might choose.

The first thing to do is to decide upon the effect which you intend to create. Next, experiment with various ways of producing it. As you can see, this picture will require both thought and imagination.

5

OUR WORLD OF COLOR

WHEREVER YOU may be as you read this page, it is very likely that there are colors within sight which you cannot name. Look about you. What is the color of the wall? The floor? The chair upon which you are sitting? If your answer is brown, or gray, or green, can you tell how this particular hue of brown, gray, or green differs from hundreds of other browns, grays, or greens? Can you tell a yellowish brown from a reddish brown? A blue-green from a yellow-green?

Do You Know Colors When You See Them?

If you are asked the color of the sky on a fair day in summer, your answer will most probably be, blue. This answer is only partially correct. Look at the sky some fine day and you will find that blue sky near the horizon is slightly greenish. As your eye moves upward toward the zenith, you will find that the blue changes into pure blue, and finally shades into a violet blue overhead.

Have you heard the story of the farmer who objected to the color of the distant hills in the artist's picture? He said to the artist, "Why do you make those hills blue? They are green. I've been over there and I know!" The artist asked him to do a little experi-

75

ment. "Bend over and look at the hills between your legs." As the farmer did this, the artist asked, "Now what color are the hills?" The farmer looked again, then he stood up and looked. "By gosh, they turned blue!" he said.

It is quite possible that you have looked at many colors which you did not really recognize. Sky is not just blue; it is many kinds of blue. Grass is not plain green; it may be one of several varieties of green. A red brick wall frequently is not pure red. It may vary from yellow-orange to violet-red in color, but to the unseeing eye it is just red brick.

> Check up on your own ability to see colors. Let each member of the class write the name or names of the colors found in the exterior of your school building. Hand in your papers to one person and have the color names read. How well do they agree? If members of the class do not agree, is it because they have not observed accurately, or because they do not know the right color names?

Do You Enjoy Beautiful Color?

Color surrounds us. We cannot escape it, but whether we enjoy it or not depends on our ability to see. Some people enjoy colors only when they are brilliant and spectacular like a burst of fireworks on the Fourth of July. Other people also enjoy colors that are quiet and lovely like sunlight on a young birch tree. It is a great deal of fun to be able to see and enjoy fine color harmonies wherever we may find them, in the woods, in the sky, on the street, in a rug, or in a necktie. This kind of enjoyment costs nothing and if it helps to make life more pleasant, why not make the most of it?

Study of Color Theory Helps

A study of color theory may sound like a very dull way to learn how to enjoy color. Nevertheless, this kind of study *does* help us to observe and enjoy beautiful color. This study consists mostly of playing with colors and hunting for color harmonies. It requires no skill in painting or scientific knowledge of the quantum theory —only good eyes and the ability to discover and enjoy the color in the world around us.

Color Families

For convenience, color may be dvided into six families— yellow, orange, red, violet, blue, green. Beginning with yellow at the top of the circle, let your gaze move slowly around the middle circle and note the color changes. Try the same thing with the tints in the outer circle. You will find that there is an intermediate color between each two main colors, for example, blue-green between blue and green and so on. These in-between colors are all related to their neighboring colors or families.

All the colors in the world which our eyes can perceive belong to one of the six families shown on the color circle. Immediately you will begin to think of colors which do not seem to belong to the yellow, orange, red, violet, blue, or green families. What about black? Gray? White? It is true that black, gray, and white do not belong to any of the six color families. They are called neutrals. Here is really the character which distinguishes one color. A real black is total darkness; in other words, an absence of color. A real white is total brightness; that is, light from the sun. Gray is the neutral which lies somewhere in between white and black.

Did you ever have a blue dress or shirt that faded? When it was washed or hung in the sun it lost its distinctive color, and became gray or white. Now you can see why black, white, and gray are called neutrals, but not colors.

Next you may ask, what about brown, taupe, olive green, and

jade? Let us study the differences in the three color circles on page 80A. The middle circle contains bright colors. They are as bright as can be made with printer's ink. If we were to see them in a rainbow or as colored lights, they would, of course, be still brighter. When colors are very brilliant we say that the *intensity* is high. When the highest possible intensity occurs in colors, as in colored lights, we call them *spectrum* colors. (We also speak of the brightest colors produced with paints or printer's inks as spectrum colors, although they are not truly of spectrum intensity.) The spectrum colors are produced when the light rays from the sun pass through rain drops and the white light is dispersed into rays of different colors and wave length. If you have a glass prism, you can make rainbow colors by letting sunlight pass through it.

The colors in the outer circle page 80A are lighter than the spectrum colors in the middle circle. They are also less intense. These pale colors, sometimes called tints or pastels, were made by adding white to the spectrum hues. In this case, the white was added by using less color on a white background, which actually shows through the thin film of color. We are all familiar with the color names which are given to tints—pink, lavender, sky blue, coral. Can you think of others?

The colors in the inner circle (page 80A) are neutralized tones, or less intense than the spectrum colors. The bright spectrum hues have been grayed or neutralized. There are two ways of neutralizing colors when you are using paints: by adding white, gray or black; or by adding the color complement. *Color complements are always directly across the color circle from each other.* You will see that yellow and violet are directly opposite. The neutralized tones of yellow and violet shown in the inner circle were made by adding a little of their color complements to each hue. Yellow was added to violet, producing the grayed violet; and violet was added to the yellow, producing the dull yellow in the inner circle. Notice that the neutralized tones of yellow-orange, orange, and red-orange, shown in the inner circle, vary from khaki-tan to a warm, rust shade.

Hues, Values, and Intensity

As you learn more about using colors, you will begin to think in terms of hue, value, and intensity. When you select your clothing, you want to choose colors that are becoming to you. You can do this most successfully if you understand the characteristics of different colors—hue, value, and intensity. You are more or less familiar with the meaning of these words, but you should know exactly what they mean when used to describe color.

Hue is that property of a color by which its part of the spectrum is distinguished—as red, blue, yellow, or violet. It may seem that hue and color mean the same thing, but this is not entirely true. If you were asked to describe the *color* pink, you would have to say that the *hue* is red, but you cannot give a full description until you state its value (light red), and you would further describe it by giving its intensity (weak or strong).

Value is that property of a color which gives it lightness or darkness. For example, spectrum red has middle value between white and black. Pink is a light value and maroon is a dark value. There are many gradations in value as between a very light, delicate pink and a darker pink.

Intensity is that property of a color which gives it strength or brightness of hue. Adding neutral to a color reduces its intensity. The more neutral that is added, the less intense (more dull) the color becomes.

It is important to recognize and understand differences in hue, value, and intensity as you observe the world about you. There are scientific instruments that can measure these variations in color with great accuracy. There is no need for you to learn this science in order to use and enjoy color in your everyday life. But if you are to get maximum pleasure from color, you must train your eye to detect the small differences in hues, values, and intensities which are important in achieving fine color harmonies. Following are some suggestions for experimenting with water colors. These experiments should help you to see different effects which can be produced by using varying hues, values, and intensities.

Play with water colors to see what tints, shades, and intermediate tones you can produce. Try to make ivory, tan, coral, orchid, jade, brown, maroon, olive green, and rose-pink. Use only spectrum colors, and black, white, or gray paint. Adding water is one way of making a color lighter, but the effect is different from that produced by adding white. It is not worth while to spend much time making a color circle. It is better to play with the paints, making spots of color. You might label each spot, telling how you secured the effect.

An experiment to do: Try neutralizing each of the six colors with its complement. Start with orange. First make a spot of bright orange on your paper, then below this make another spot of bright orange but while the paint is still wet, add a little bright blue to the orange. Below this spot make a third spot in which there is still more blue and less orange. In doing this experiment you will certainly see how orange can be neutralized by adding its complement, blue.

Repeat this experiment with each of the other colors, red, violet, blue, green, and yellow. In each case add the color complement. Use no neutrals.

Compare the effects obtained by neutralizing a color with a neutral—black, gray, or white—and neutralizing the same color with its color complement. In which case does the neutralized tone seem more alive and interesting? In which case does it seem less bright and somewhat lifeless?

The middle circle shows strong, bright colors (spectrum hues). The outer circle shows how each color changes when white is added, making a pale blue instead of a bright blue, a pink instead of bright red, and so on. The inner circle shows what happens when each color is grayed or made less intense. We sometimes speak of these colors as tones or shades.

Note: Study of colors should always be carried on under daylight. Artificial light affects the hue in some colors. For example, blue may look slightly greenish under artificial light.

BUFFET GROUP, DESIGNED BY DON WALLANCE FOR THE FORECAST
COLLECTION OF ALUMINUM COMPANY OF AMERICA

*These aluminum housewares were designed with thought for both beauty
and functional quality. Further discussion of their art quality and usefulness are found on pages 83 and 84.*

80B

Accidental Minglings Are Fun to Do

One of the best ways to enjoy color is to play with it. Try mingling two or more colors, allowing them to mix as they will. Drop some water color paint on white drawing paper and allow it to flow freely. Try wetting the paper first and dropping the paint on it. (It should not be so wet that it will run off the paper.) While it is still wet, drop another color into it and let the colors blend to make an accidental mingling. Pick the paper up, tip it, and guide the flow. Use your brush as little as possible.

Using Hue, Value, and Intensity to Create Beauty

The display of the household items in the illustration shown on page 80B was skillfully arranged to create an interesting and harmonious color effect. Tables, casseroles, a hors d'oeuvre tree, salad bowl, serving spoon, and the fruits, eggs, and vegetables are placed so as to make an interesting pattern. Obviously, it is not planned as a table setting, but rather as an arrangement of beautiful objects designed for use in twentieth-century homes.

The picture provides an opportunity to study pleasing color combinations. The artist who arranged the display knows how to use hues, values, and intensities to produce a lovely effect. Our eyes go first to the brilliant colors of the relish dishes supported by the arms of the hors d'oeuvre tree. From this center of interest, our gaze moves back across the table tops to the very edge of the picture. What causes this feeling of looking back to the farthermost table? It is chiefly a matter of color values and intensities.

The most intense colors are found in the group of relish plates and the grapes. As your eye moves back into the picture, the colors gradually become less intense. The yellow of the apple on the last table is very pale compared to the yellows in the relish dishes. Now study the color values. The blue tablecloth on the first table is a much darker value than the light yellow one on the last table. The intense colors of the relish dishes are seen against the tablecloth of dark, low-intensity blue, which makes an excellent background. Do you think the colors of these dishes would have seemed as beautiful if they had been placed on one of the other tablecloths?

Remember that a background, whether it is a tablecloth or the wall of a room, should not overwhelm or "fight" with the things which are seen in front of it. When you select the color for a background, think carefully about hue, value, and intensity.

Understanding Color Harmonies

Our world of color is full of harmonies. You will find them in flowers, trees, shells, in window draperies, paintings, magazines, and numberless other examples. You will also find disharmonious effects almost anywhere!

Your study of color harmony includes two main problems— (1) how to recognize harmonious effects when you see them, and (2) how to create good harmonies. There are no exact rules for creating color harmonies, but your knowledge of hues, values, and intensities will help. There are many occasions in everyday life when you will wish to combine colors harmoniously. Perhaps you will be planning a new spring outfit consisting of a suit, shirt, shoes, tie and socks. Or if you are a girl, it may be a dress, coat, hat, gloves and shoes. Naturally you wish to have a good-looking ensemble, and color is an important factor. Or you may be planning new curtains for your room. What color will harmonize with the other furnishings?

Understanding color harmonies help solve such problems as these. You made a start in learning how to harmonize colors while considering the picture on page 80B. There the colors seem to belong together—they show off each other's beauty, as in the case of the brilliant dishes on the neutral blue tablecloth.

A good general rule to follow in selecting harmonious colors is to try them out on the eye. The colors should look as though they belong together.

Plan a class session for experiments in combining colors harmoniously. Assemble a collection of colors from home—papers, cloths, china, and other items. Your teacher will probably have a collection of colored papers which can be used. First try combinations of two colors, and then three colors. Stay with not more than three colors until you gain experience. Remember to *try it on the eye.*

Monochromatic or Self-Tone Harmonies

The simplest type of color harmony is the monochromatic or self-tone harmony, which consists of varying values and intensities of *one hue.* For example, a cotton print curtain material or a summer dress fabric might have a light tan background with the floral pattern in tones of orange and brown. These colors all belong to the orange family, so they all have something in common and are not likely to disagree.

Anyone of the twelve colors on the color circle can be used for a monochromatic harmony, and any neutral, black, white, or gray may be used with it. Since neutrals have no color, they can be added to the self-tone harmony without changing the color scheme.

If you were making a monochromatic mingling with orange paint, you might use neutrals to mix with the spectrum orange to produce the neutral tones such as tan, brown, beige, ecru, and other tones, or you might prefer to use the complement of orange, which is blue. In this case, you would not allow the pure blue or bluish tones to show in the mingling, but use only enough blue to produce dull orange, and the brownish colors.

Monochromatic color schemes are often used in dress. A girl might plan an outfit with a blue coat and hat, dark blue shoes, a white hat and gloves, a blue and white print dress with a white collar, and perhaps a blue or white purse. A boy might choose a brown suit, sox, and shoes; tan, brown or white shirts to wear for changes; and orange, brown, or figured ties.

You will observe many examples of monochromatic harmonies in nature. The English sparrow with his brownish back and wings, black throat, gray breast and white markings is rather dull in appearance, partly because of the coating of city dirt which he often acquires! The blue jay, with his bright blue feathers and black and white markings, wears a much more striking monochromatic harmony.

> Be prepared to report examples of monochromatic harmonies which you have seen in nature, pictures, or elsewhere.

Adjacents or Neighboring Colors Make Fine Harmonies

The colors which lie near to each other on the color circle are called adjacents. Yellow has yellow-green on one side and yellow-orange on the other. The next two neighbors are orange and green as you go around the circle. Two or more of these neighboring colors may be used to create an adjacent harmony. Yellow jonquils have lovely yellow petals and yellow-green stems and leaves. Some have orange centers. The coloring of leaves in the fall often contains adjacent harmonies in yellows and greens, reds and yellows.

You will find several groups of neighboring colors on the circle which produce beautiful harmonies when blended, such as the orange-red, red, and red violet coloring which may appear in a sunset. An autumn leaf, just beginning to turn color, may show tones of green, yellow-green, and yellow.

You will enjoy making accidental minglings of two or three adjacents. Some of the loveliest harmonies are made from delicate tints of neighboring colors.

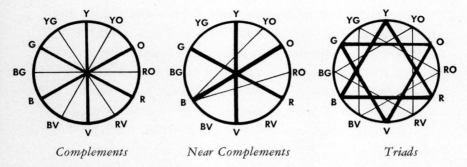

Complements   *Near Complements*   *Triads*

Watch for examples of adjacent harmonies as you go about your daily routine. If possible, bring examples to class.

Complementary Colors Can Be Harmonized

Color complements are always directly across the circle from each other. The first diagram below shows you six pairs of complementary colors. Notice that the connecting lines pass through the center of the circle. The color names are represented by their first letters—Y for yellow, YO for yellow-orange, and so on. Learn the position of each color so that you can remember the color complements without referring to the circle —also the six pairs of color complements.

Complementary colors have a much more difficult time getting along with each other than do adjacent colors. They are opposite colors—just as far away from each other on the circle as possible. They are strangers. They are like people of two different lands who have nothing in common. For example, bright red and brilliant green used together produce just about as disagreeable an effect as one can find in color combinations. But reds and greens of different values and intensities used together produce a very lovely effect. Pink roses and their green leaves make a delightful harmony. Another nice red and green combination is the red berries and dark, waxy green leaves of holly.

You will be able to think of many flowers which show lovely harmonies of the complementary colors red and green.

When nature uses complementary colors together she generally creates a harmonious effect.   Hues of spectrum intensity do not often appear together.   Almost always some of the colors in the combination are neutralized and appear as tints, tones, or shades. For example, brilliant red tulips do not have brilliant green leaves and stems.   The greens are well neutralized and have a rather silvery-green quality which combines beautifully with the brilliant red blossoms.

> Plan a table setting in which you use a pair of complementary colors. For the Christmas season, you might use red and green or for a spring party you might also use red and green.   What different values of red and green would you probably choose for the spring party?

The blue and orange pair of complements is frequently used to produce delightful harmonies.   You will see it in a great many places.   Nature uses it in a golden sunset with blue sky above, in the russet-brown oak trees against October's bright blue sky and in the blue bird's coloring.   You will see it in advertisements and in show windows.   You may even find it on your breakfast table. Can you imagine a breakfast table planned in a blue-and-orange complementary harmony?   The china is bright blue but not nearly as bright as a true spectrum blue.   The orange juice furnishes the brightest note of orange.   Other tones of orange are furnished by the table top, doilies and napkins, hot cakes, sausages, and maple syrup.   Color harmonies like this cost no more than poor color combinations, and they may even make your breakfast taste better!

A very effective blue and orange harmony is shown on page 88A.   Here you see a combination of articles made by man with various objects from nature. The lovely curtain fabrics are made from a synthetic fiber, Dacron, in combination with other fibers. The blue fabric draped over the driftwood is enhanced by the subdued patterns of stripes. Notice that in the shadows of the folds, the blue has a blue-violet touch. In comparison with this effect, you see that the fabric at the window has a distinct blue-greenish cast.

The orange colors in this complementary harmony are supplied by the shells, the starfish, the driftwood, and the brownish tan material draped upon the driftwood.

As you test the whole effect with your eye, you feel at once that it is a lovely harmony. Can you imagine how crude and raw the effect would have been if the designer had used only spectrum blue and spectrum orange? There is only one spot of very bright color in the whole arrangement—the brilliant orange seashell. This is a nice accent which adds interest to the effect, but what a mistake it would have been if the designer had used a piece of brilliant orange fabric in place of the blue-green material at the window!

Generally it is best in creating a color harmony to use intense color in small areas.

The third pair of complementary colors with which you should be acquainted is the yellow and violet combination. This harmony has limited use. Yet in many instances, you will see the yellow and violet combination used beautifully. Think of yellow and violet pansies, violets with yellow centers, or an orchid tied with pale yellow ribbon.

Report to the class any examples of complementary harmonies that you have seen recently. Note whether the colors were bright or well neutralized. If possible, bring samples of complementary harmonies to class.

A variation of the complementary color scheme is produced by using near-complements as shown in the second diagram on page 85. In this instance, the neighboring colors red-orange and yellow-orange are used instead of orange as a complement to the blue. Sometimes only one near-complement might be used, perhaps the red-orange as shown in the picture on page 88A.

Many different kinds of effects can be obtained by using the near complements.

> Experiment with accidental minglings of complementary colors—also with near-complements. Plan for a classroom exhibit of the best results. (Remember that intermediate tones result from mingling (neutralizing) a color with its complement.)

Triads—Three-Color Harmonies

The third diagram on page 85 shows the triad combinations on the color circle. Look first at the triangle with heavy lines which points to red, yellow, and blue. These three colors are sometimes called the primary colors. The other triangle made with heavy lines, points to orange, green, and violet. This trio of colors consists of secondary colors. The two triangles drawn with light lines point out suggestions for other triad color combinations.

You will see triad harmonies both in nature and art. You may see the western sky blazing with color—fiery reds and yellows at the heart of the sunset, fading off into blue sky at the edges. In between will be many intermediate colors, but chiefly a red-yellow-blue effect.

The color illustration on page 88D is based on the red-yellow-blue triad. The burnished, yellow tones of the cross and candlesticks, and the gleaming yellow lights seen against the darkness of the background, produce a moving, and dramatic effect. The glowing red of the ledge which supports the candlesticks is a per-

The curtain materials shown in the display arrangement above are made from blends of Dacron and other fibers. The lovely color effect is created by the combination of complementary blue and orange, in tones which blend harmoniously. The faint pattern of stripes in the fabrics provides a nice suggestion of textures, and the light falls across the folds of the drapery so as to produce added interest.

88A

88B

THE "COLLECTOR'S GROUP" OF CABIN CRAFTS RUGS
COURTESY, CABIN CRAFTS, INC.

This handsome color advertisement suggests good-humored refinement and taste. Carefully harmonized colors lend an air of elegance. Obviously the gentleman in the picture is used to having only the best. Doesn't his attitude suggest that this group of rugs is out of the ordinary? See page 104.

Nature produces wonderful color harmonies. The lovely blue-violet, violet, and red violet tones of the grapes, the yellow-greens, greens, and blue-greens of the leaves, and the red-orange of the stems and little spots on the leaves are blended into a very successful harmony.

88C

ALTAR GROUP, DESIGNED BY RAMBUSCH STUDIOS, FOR THE FORECAST
COLLECTION OF ALUMINUM COMPANY OF AMERICA

*Function as well as beauty were considered in the design of the aluminum
altar pieces shown above. We are likely to think of aluminum as gray-
silver, but it can now be produced in many colors by a process called
anodizing. The cross and candlesticks were designed with beautiful simplicity. The tall, slender shapes create a pleasing vertical movement, and
the circular shapes of the bases and catch plates provide a pleasant contrast.
Functional features include weighted bases which prevent the candlesticks
from tipping over easily. The cups which hold the candles are removable,
thus making it simple to install fresh candles. The catch plates are also
removable, making it a simple matter to clean off the candle drippings.*

88D

fect foil for the yellow tones. Notice how the red is reflected into the golden hue of the candlesticks and how the golden metal is reflected upon the surface of the brilliant red counter.

Both the reds and the yellows are echoed in the background. It may seem to you that the background is merely black, but if you study it carefully you will see that there are hints of blue throughout and that reds, yellows, violet and green are mingled in the darkness.

Tips on Color Harmonies

1. Beware of combinations of two or more very intense colors. They are not likely to get on well together.

2. Use intense color in small areas. Brilliant colors in large areas are likely to outshine and overwhelm the harmony.

3. Decide on the type of color harmony you want before you begin work. Do you want it to be bold and exciting? Delicate and lovely? Quiet? Noisy? After you have decided what you want, then plan your colors accordingly. *To be sure, try it on the eye.*

EXPERIENCES IN APPRECIATION

1. Make a color notebook. Collect samples of different types of color harmonies and label and classify them on the pages of your notebook. You will find color harmonies in magazine illustrations, advertisements, leaves and flowers which can be pressed and mounted, fabrics, wallpaper, etc.

2. Arrange a series of bulletin-board exhibitions. From the samples of color which members of the class contribute and from the teacher's illustrative material, arrange exhibitions of different harmonies, one with neutrals, adjacents, complementaries, and triads.

3. Hold a color contest. The teacher will arrange several examples of color combinations on the bulletin board and about the classroom. These will consist of color prints, textiles, and other design materials. Each sample will bear a number. The class will then attempt to identify the pre-

dominant color scheme in each sample. Each member will write down his answer for each number. Then compare answers and see what score you made.

4. Collect samples of colored fabrics. These may be satin, chiffon, cheesecloth, or any other kind of fabric. Collect as many different samples of color as possible. Practice combining these samples to make pleasing color harmonies. Let two or three people combine the colors while the rest of the class criticizes.

5. Try the accidental minglings described in the first problem under "Creative Activities." It does require the use of paint but no particular skill. Anyone can do it and enjoy playing with color.

CREATIVE ACTIVITIES

1. Use water colors to make some accidental minglings of various color combinations. In making an accidental mingling do not try to make a picture of anything. Merely let your colors flow together in interesting arrangements.

a. Try each pair of complements mingled to make a light, delicate effect, and a dark, rich effect.

b. Try red with its adjacents, blue with its adjacents, and yellow with its adjacents.

c. Try the red-yellow-blue triad to show a harmonious effect. Remember to let one color predominate.

d. Try the same with the orange-green-violet triad.

2. Experiment with colors to express emotions, moods, and certain types of occasions. For example, you might choose reds, yellows, and purples splashed on your paper in forceful brush strokes to express anger. Or you might choose grays and lovely, quiet blues and greens to express serenity. For Independence Day, you might use reds, whites, blues, and other strong colors to express the idea of the day.

3. Hold a class discussion in which each person suggests an idea that might be expressed with colors. You will find it best to use water colors or poster paints for this project. Do not try to draw a picture or design. Merely use your colors in free, "accidental" minglings.

4. Make a set of color cards for colored paper. Use as many colors as you can find. Experiment with these cards to "discover" how different colors, tints, and shades change your mood. Which ones make you feel gay and happy? Cool? Sad? Warm?

6

ART GOES INTO BUSINESS

Do YOU RECALL your discovery of beautiful forms in trees, water, and clouds, and the fine, strong lines in the horse? Remember some of the ways color is used to produce certain results? You may ask, "Well, what does all this lead up to?" You might say it's just a way to have more fun. Or you may decide that each of the things you studied had a meaning for some future use. Be on the watch for beauty in art and nature everywhere.

Perhaps you have thought of each chapter in this book as a separate form of art. Yet learning about design and color from different approaches leads to better choice of clothing, or points out how to improve your ideas in home decorating. Your knowledge of color and design helps you to decide which combinations are the right ones. As you begin to observe things around you in a new, fresh way, you also begin to discriminate between the ordinary and the fine. This is called development of taste. The development of good taste is the result of all your art experiences. Good taste means that your choices fit the need, please others, and give long satisfaction.

Manufacturers know about the development of good taste, too. They hire artists to design their products so people will approve them. How often have you said, "Oh, I like that. It looks good!"

You may be speaking of a watch, a record player, a box of cereal, or an automobile! You like these things first of all for their *appearance.* In Chapter 2 you read about the industrial designer, who designs automobiles. He might also design electric toasters, refrigerators, or chairs, as well as the other items listed above. So you see, art really "goes into business."

Let Art Sell It

Let's suppose a manufacturer has produced a line of well-designed toasters, ladders, or chairs. Now he must market them. This is where the smart business man says, "Let art sell it!" You can readily see that the artist plays a big part here. He designs posters, circulars, signs, and advertising layouts for magazines and newspapers. He creates animated TV commercial art and "stage settings."

Here again, good taste is important, since we know that the chief purpose of an advertisement is to catch the attention of the reader and persuade him to buy the product. Many advertisers do not know that it's easier to attract attention and make a favorable impression by emphasizing one center of interest through orderly arrangements than to crowd as many things as possible into a limited space. You can easily make a comparison of a simple, orderly arrangement with a crowded, cluttered one. Next time you walk through a shopping district, look at the display windows of several stores along the street. You're sure to see some uncluttered, *tastefully* arranged displays. And close by, you're certain to see some which appear to be a hodge-podge of all the items in the store! The owner of this latter store doesn't realize that such a condition of disorder serves only to confuse the passerby. The store owner who carefully and tastefully displays only "lead" items which belong with each other is actually telling the shopper that there are many more fine things inside, displayed as serviceably as those in the window. This is a subtle invitation to come in and look for them.

In some instances, it is better not to use any advertising. If an advertisement creates a bad impression, it is not likely to persuade people to buy. Compare the two highways below for beauty. Obviously the upper one is far more attractive than the other, which is marred by ugly signboards. People who enjoy driving through beautiful country on good roads cannot help but be annoyed by billboards which mar and interfere with the land-

COURTESY NATIONAL ROADSIDE COUNCIL

scape. They will not be persuaded to buy products advertised on billboards which destroy the loveliness of the countryside.

Packages Sell the Products

On page 94, you read that the purpose of advertising is to catch the attention of the reader and persuade him to buy the product. Do you agree that the product may be its own best advertisement? Isn't this true of automobiles? Wouldn't it also apply to furniture, household appliances, or a box of cereal? A product advertises itself by its *appearance*. No matter how many words we might write about something, if it's not good looking people don't want it. Have you ever looked closely at the boxes, envelopes, and packages that contain products you or your parents buy? Many of these are planned with great care. A well-designed, attractively colored package suggests a high quality product inside. Some products are identified by their package designs. Which brands of breakfast cereal can you identify by the package design?

Packages of the future may be quite different from those of today. New materials will increase the possibilities for greater beauty and utility alike. On the opposite page are pictured two delightful new package designs made of aluminum foil and paper board. These packages do not appear to be billboards-in-miniature, as others often do. Created by a group of industrial designers, these sparkling containers encourage a prospective buyer to select their contents purely because of the beauty and usefulness of the package.

Another container design is a fascinating cube which separates into six individual modular, or similar, pyramids. It might be useful for ice cream, or perhaps cheese, with the package dividing into six servings. Wouldn't it be fun to serve ice cream to your friends in this manner? Just peel back those sides and dig in!

The attractive containers above are for dry products, such as candy, soap powder, or perhaps salt, in the smaller size. The graceful, fluted drum container allows for perforations or a turn top for dispensing contents. The tripod containers below are ideally suited for milk or soft drinks. Picture your milk served in this clever style.

Do you see how a well-designed package can "catch on"? Let's see now, cream-yellow foil for vanilla, green for mint—you supply the others!

This interesting package would be purchased in a cube shape. It opens out into six individual servings. Choose your favorite ice cream flavor by the color of the section!

Choose a day when each member of the class will bring the most interesting package he can find. Discuss the attractive and functional qualities in each of these containers.

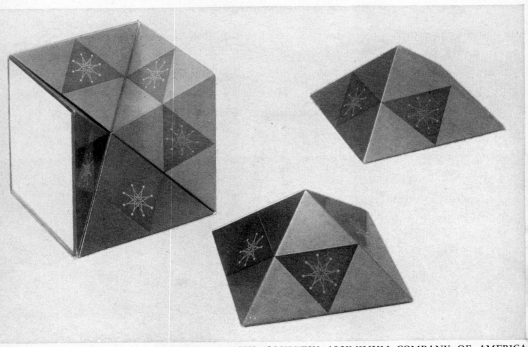

PHOTO COURTESY ALUMINUM COMPANY OF AMERICA

Emphasis says "Look!"

The chief importance of an advertisement is to catch the attention of the public and tell about a product or service. To do this, the advertisement must be emphatic or forceful. What's the first thing you see when you look at the ad below? Of course it's the

NEW SIZE 4x12

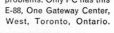

We thought of a lot of fancy names for this new PC glass product. But they seemed considerably less articulate than the quiet simplicity of the product itself. We settled on what seemed natural—the **4x12.** The outside faces are smooth for practical reasons. But an acid-etched appearance gives character and texture to the interior faces. The product is available with a white insert screen, a green-tinted screen, or plain. And, of course, there's color. At present, four ceramic face hues, with more to come. But most important—the new size—**4x12.** A break with tradition that gives architects a new proportion in solving design problems. Only PC has this product, so call or write. Pittsburgh Corning Corporation, Dept. E-88, One Gateway Center, Pittsburgh 22, Pa. In Canada: 57 Bloor Street West, Toronto, Ontario.

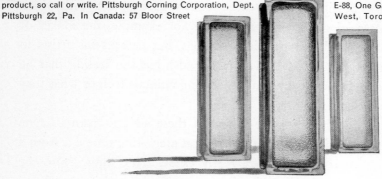

PITTSBURGH CORNING

large block of numerals at the top, and the words "New Size" directly above. Do you see how the artist made a compact design of the words and numerals so that one quick glance would tell the story? This outsized block was deliberately made very large and dark in order to emphasize a single, significant characteristic of a product. With such pronounced emphasis, the reader will be moved to look further to discovery why the numbers are so large. The explanation under the numbers tells the rest of the story briefly. This ad was designed to sell a new size of glass block to builders, and it was printed in several builders' magazines.

There are probably some advertisements you have seen that are more familiar to you. Some advertisers use the same picture, or the same kind of picture, several times, so that readers get to know the product through recognition of the ad. This is a different kind of emphasis, but the result is the same—to make the reader take notice.

Let's Get Personal

In advertising, it's often a good idea to get as "close" to the reader as possible. To do this, the artist uses subjects with which the potential customer is familiar. For example, the maker of Ideal dog food uses drawings of dogs, but he asks his artists to give them personality! The reader also has the feeling that he knows just how the amusing, charming animals feel, or what they are thinking.

On the following page is one of these advertisements. One can't miss the idea that the dog and cat are taking time out from a feud to eat something they really enjoy. We know from the picture that the dog is anxious to eat, anxious enough to stop doing something else he also enjoys—fighting with the cat! The artist suggests that *your* dog will be every bit as eager to eat at this one!

COURTESY, WILSON & COMPANY

Emphasis Is a Principle of Art

This principle of art called emphasis is important in all kinds of art. It will help you to plan a poster, arrange a room, or paint a picture. It will help you think of the most important thing in your arrangement. Art arrangements that lack emphasis on a center of interest are generally not as successful as those that are built around a center of interest, or *center of emphasis.*

Advertising and Emotion

You may wonder how these two words, advertising and emotion, are related. But if you realize that your feelings about things are really emotions, you will see how an advertisement "uses" them. The ad below shows how the artist makes our emotions work to help sell the idea or product. This was designed for the television series, "I Remember Mama." The artist's task was to create a desire in the reader to watch the programs. This he

COURTESY, THOROFARE MARKETS, INC. AGENCY,
KETCHUM, MCLEOD & GROVE, INC.

accomplished by appealing to emotion, using the rocking chair, knitting basket, and footstool, things which the reader recognizes as belonging to "Mama." The emotion is sentiment. Recalled to mind are the many enjoyable times we had together, perhaps watching "Mama" make candy, or helping her wrap sandwiches for a family picnic. This advertisement is actually aimed at the age level of your mothers and fathers, so the "Mama" we're talking about here is your grandmother! But look at the picture again. Can you feel what it's saying to you? Would you like to see a program based on your mother's times—the 1940's and 50's, or her earlier years, the '20's and '30's?

Color Can Make or Break

The right color is tremendously important in making an advertisement pleasing and emphatic. It has been proved by scientific investigation that some color combinations can be seen at much greater distance than others. Black letters on a yellow background can be read further than any other combination of colors. Yellow light rays have greater penetrating power than any other. That is why the center lines on highways in states are painted yellow instead of white. The yellow lines show in fog and at night.

Of course, we do not wish to use only black and yellow. But it is important that colors have enough contrast to be seen and read easily. When choosing colors for an advertisement, think first of the conditions involved. If your advertisement is to be read from a distance, choose colors that are legible from a distance. If the advertisement is to be read close at hand, then more subtle color combinations may be used. Be certain to choose colors that are harmonious. Good color combinations are pleasant, and they make good impressions. Unpleasant color combinations will not make a good impression, and people will not be persuaded to buy. The study of color in Chapter 5 should help you think of many color combinations that are both legible and harmonious.

Color Photographs in Advertising

Sometimes the advertiser wants the observer to see his product in its true color and in a real setting. The advertisement may then be made from a color photograph. This is a very expensive process, so the advertiser who uses it attempts to make the reader see his product in the best possible setting.

Sometimes advertisers crowd too many things into one layout, and the refinement that he might get with color is lost. Other advertisers know that a carefully planned color ad can be very complimentary to their products. This often means using few colors, selected to suggest quality and good taste. The advertisement back on page 88C is a fine example of careful color selection, lending an air of high status to the product. The distinguished, well-dressed gentleman looking over the selection is obviously interested only in the very best! His sophistication and expensive good taste suggest that these rugs are truly "collectors" items. Have you noticed the background color? This soft gray tone was probably the most thoughtfully selected color in the scene. Can you tell why? Why are the walls and floor the same color?

There are two things about this advertisement you should notice especially: (1) Take note of the restraint used in the selection of colors. Did you realize that only two colors are used in the rugs? They are red and orange, in various intensities and values. Black is used here and there for contrast. The artist knew that by selecting only a few colors, the reader could fully appreciate their subtle differences. Actually, this is another form of emphasis, isn't it? (2) Note the unusual arrangement. Hanging the rugs on the wall draws attention to them because this is not the way we usually see rugs. Remember these points. Look for similar examples in other advertisements.

Do you think closely related colors (adjacents) or opposite colors make the best effect on posters? Why or why not?

Do you think a combination of light and dark values or light and middle values makes a more legible combination? Why?

Study Your Newspaper and Magazine Advertisements

There are a great many advertisements in our newspapers and magazines. The purpose of each advertisement is to sell a product or an idea, but some of them are more successful than others. Readers of newspapers and magazines do not have time to read all advertisements. They read only those which attract their attention and are easy to read. Try an experiment. Take a magazine which has several pages of advertising and turn through the pages without looking for any special thing. Which advertisements caught your eye and interested you enough so that you read the whole advertisement? Next ask several members of your class to do the same thing. How many of you noticed the same advertisements? You will probably find that the same advertisements are forceful enough to catch the attention of most readers.

Next analyze these advertisements and try to find out why they caught your attention. Do you find a successful use of the art principles, emphasis, rhythm, proportions, and balance?

Collect newspaper and magazine advertisements. Select those which you consider the most effective advertisements. Analyze each one of the ads for the use of art principles. For example, which one do you consider shows the best use of the principle of emphasis? The most effective use of color?

Good Lettering Is Important

All kinds of advertisements carry at least a few words, and the lettering in these words can do a great deal to make the advertisement forceful and attractive. If the lettering is poor, it may make the poster both ugly and hard to read. On the other hand if the lettering is good, it makes the poster more beautiful and easier to understand.

Sometimes an advertisement is made up of lettering alone. This can be very interesting or very dull, depending on how inventive the artist is. Letters can be grouped to form designs, or their shapes and sizes changed so that they fit together as a unit. Of course, the style of lettering must suit the use for which it is intended. The name plate below is a good example of catchy design in letters. It was used to advertise a commercial art studio. Striking contrasts attract the reader's attention. The interesting sizes and lively shape and arrangement of the letters make this an outstanding example of pure lettering design.

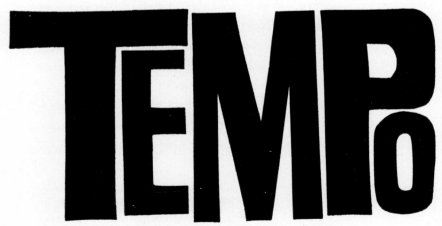

ATlantic 1-0980-81-82 Granite Building, 6th & Wood, Pittsburgh 22, Pennsylvania

COURTESY, TEMPO

Now You Try It!

Everyone should know how to make good printed letters in at least one style of alphabet. There are many occasions in anyone's life when it is handy to know how to letter a few words. You may need this skill for your maps and diagrams in other school subjects. There are frequent uses for lettering. At the beginning of this book we said that it is not necessary for everyone to draw well in order to understand and enjoy art. However, lettering is one kind of technical work that does not require great art talent. If you wish, you can learn to do good lettering.

Styles of Alphabets

Here are a few styles of alphabets with which you should become familiar. The simplest one is shown below. It is a single-line alphabet that is suitable for use in lettering maps, charts, diagrams, and small posters. In this style of alphabet each line is made with a single stroke of the pen or pencil. For charts or maps it is best to use a pen or pencil that makes a thin line, but for posters or signs it is best to use a heavy crayon or pen with a broad,

ABCD aabcd
abcdef ABCDEFGHI

A simple alphabet that's easy to make with a small, round nibbed pen.

flat nib.   Some of the flat-nibbed pens have very broad disks and these are specially suitable for lettering signs or posters quickly.

Oversize letters are often drawn first, then filled in.   The professional artist uses a very light guideline, then draws his letters directly onto the poster board.   He may use chalk or light pencil lines so that he can make changes easily.   With some practice you can make clean-looking block letters such as shown below.   Why don't you try?   This kind of letter looks best when it's quite large. Often these letters are drawn on squared paper and then transferred to the poster.

ABCDEFG
ABCDabc

Use block letters like these for posters and other large signs.

Another style of alphabet with which you should be familiar is a very old one.   It was first used by the Romans on their great monuments, and so it is known as the Roman alphabet.   The letters were first drawn on the stone and then cut with a chisel. A great many modern alphabets are patterned after this old Roman alphabet.   Sometimes the letters are made with lines varying in thickness and with different proportions, but they are based on the Roman style.   Most of our books are printed with a style of alphabet derived from the Roman.

This style of alphabet is not easy to use for quick lettering because the letters must be carefully drawn and correctly proportioned.   Even though you do not expect to become skillful in using the Roman alphabet, it will be profitable for you to try making a few Roman-letter forms. In this way you will become better acquainted with the style and will recognize it when you see it.

A B C D E F G H I J K L M N O P Q R S T U V W X Y Z

An alphabet based on the old Roman style.

Beauty in the Printed Page

While we are discussing beauty in letter forms, we should also think of beauty in the printed page. Letters should not only have beautiful forms, but should also be arranged well on the page. Good spacing between letters, between words, between paragraphs, and in the margins is of the utmost importance in securing a fine effect.

The arrangement made with blocks of letters and surrounding spaces should be thought of as page designs. We have learned that people are more apt to be impressed by simply designed, well-arranged displays than by cluttered, carelessly arranged ones. How can this knowledge help you in your written schoolwork? Discuss with others.

Greetings to Our Friends

Christmas, New Year's, Valentine's Day, Easter, on birthdays —these are times when we send greetings to our friends. Every year the people of the United States send millions of greeting cards as tokens of good wishes. Most of these cards are inexpensive, many of them costing only a nickel. But even they may be very attractive. Our special problem as buyers of greeting cards is to select those cards which are most charming, which say in the best possible way what we want them to. Here again our study of art will help us.

What's the Occasion?

We've talked about the principles of art in designing automobiles, advertisements, and in painting. Those same principles apply to selection of greeting cards. We'll be more satisfied with cards that are well proportioned and show good taste in color selection. But there's another principle that is involved which we must consider first of all: greeting cards are designed to suit a special occasion. Since a greeting card is meant to express good wishes at a particular season, or for a special occasion, the decoration should suggest the season of the year, or should be closely associated with the occasion. For instance, Christmas cards generally include such ideas as Christmas trees, churches, angels, winter landscapes, Santa Claus and his reindeer, and the Mother and Child. Many people prefer to send cards which suggest the origin of the celebration of Christmas—Christ's birthday. The card pictured below is based on this theme.   It is a scene in a big city on Christmas Eve.   A star on a giant Christmas tree gleams aloft, and the pale moon shines through the snowy night.   Two

A Christmas card by the famous American artist, Joseph Hirsch.

people, alone in the park, gaze in wonder and reverence at the scene on this Holy night. In this Christmas card the artist has created a lovely interpretation of the famous Christmas song, "Silent Night! Holy Night!"

We choose some cards for occasions such as birthdays or weddings. Sometimes we may have to choose a card for someone who is confined by illness or an accident but is not in desperate condition. Such a person needs to be cheered up! Card companies make a line of cards especially designed for this purpose. These cartoon cards are funny because they help the ailing person make light of his burden, whatever it may be. We've chosen a popular style to illustrate the belief that one feels better if he can smile at his own ills. The cleverly drawn illustration is accompanied inside by the lines, "What some people won't do for attention!" Don't you think that this whimsical, sparkling drawing and snappy remark would have an effervescent effect on the patient? Have you ever received a funny get-well card?

We choose a card for the invalid with a special purpose in mind —to make him forget his troubles or ills for awhile. There are other occasions when we might wish to use cartoon cards, too. How about Valentine's Day, or a special birthday greeting to someone who likes a joke? You might try a humorous Mother's Day card. It works! We found a birthday card which is designed to make Dad smile. Don't forget that this is his own special day! This card we have chosen, shown on page 112, lets Dad know that he's "top man" in our house. Our choice of the proud rooster as a subject tells Dad we want him to keep on being "top man." Incidentally, we hope you've noticed that this card is not an ordinary cartoon, but a combination of clever cartooning and rich design, resulting in a delightful compliment to the Dad who receives it.

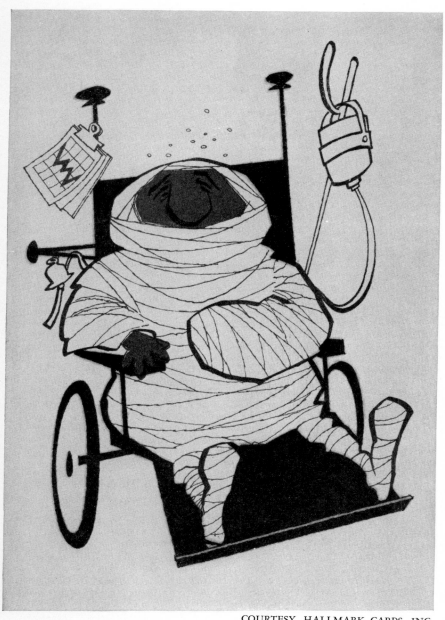

*A get-well card designed to cheer the patient. Would you
be cheered by a card like this?*

111

FROM BOTH
OF US
TO DAD

Make Your Own

Many people enjoy making their own Christmas cards, valentines, or other greeting cards. It is a good hobby. There are different ways of making them and you will enjoy trying different methods. Cards can be drawn and painted. This means that each card must be done separately and if you wish to make several it may require too much time.

One method of making greeting cards is with a linoleum print. There is not space in this book to tell you all about how to do this, but you can find out about it by consulting the books listed in the bibliography at the end of this book. Your teacher will be able to help you. The process, explained briefly, is this: A piece of linoleum the size and shape of the card is secured. The pattern is drawn upon the block. Parts of the block are cut away so that the block can be used to print the pattern on the cards. In this way a number of cards can be made quickly from one block. There were no small details to cut. If you plan to make linoleum-print Christmas cards, remember that the design should be very simple, with no fine lines and as little lettering as possible. Letters are hard to cut.

Still another way to make greeting cards is with the stencil-and-spatter method. A stencil is laid upon the card and paint is spattered over the surface. Your teacher will be able to help you work out stencils and show you how to do the spatter or brush work.

Very attractive cards are made by paper cutting—colored papers are cut and pasted with charming effects.

You may wonder how the cards sold in the stores are made. The artist makes the original drawing and colors it. This is sent to the engraver who makes line cuts or color plates which are used for printing many thousands of cards by means of the printing press.   Your drawing could be used to make a plate from which thousands of cards could be printed but it would be expensive.

EXPERIENCES IN APPRECIATION

1. Report to your class any examples of how art sells an article—in other words, how an advertisement catches the attention of the public and persuades it to buy.

2. Collect advertisements of every form—folders, cards, posters, signs, and others.   From these advertisements select the one which is the best example of the following:

    a. Emphasis

    b. Fine lettering

3. Study other styles of alphabets and collect samples.   You will find other styles of alphabets shown in the reference books listed at the end of this book.

4. Arrange for a criticism lesson on greeting cards.   First collect all the greeting cards possible.   Put them in a pile and let each member of the class select one.   Each person will criticize his card for the following points: (Remember that criticism includes good points as well as bad points.)

    1. suitability of idea, 2. treatment or character, 3. lettering

Arrange a bulletin-board exhibition of good greeting cards just before the day on which they are intended to be used.

CREATIVE ACTIVITIES

1. Letter some simple signs, using the flat-nibbed pens.

2. Make your own greeting cards for the next occasion when you wish to send cards.   Use any method which appeals to you and which your teacher thinks practical.

7

FIGURES AND FACES

IN THIS BOOK we are searching for beauty in any form that may chance to cross our paths. We have found it in automobiles, animals, trees, and advertisements. Sometimes we come upon it in objects made by man, sometimes in nature. In this search for beauty in our everyday lives, we must include a study of beauty in the human figure. Since the beginnings of art, artists have seen beauty in the human body. Figures and faces have always intrigued painters and sculptors. Some of them feel that the finest art is a representation of the human form. Countless statues and pictures of the human being have been attempted by artists both of past and present eras. Some of these statues and paintings are very beautiful and rightfully have become famous. In this chapter we shall become acquainted with some of these famous works of art in which artists have depicted beauty in the human figure and face.

We see figures and faces depicted in other ways too. One of the most common of these is the cartoon. Later on in this chapter we shall look at some cartoons, and decide how important they are in representations of the human form. A caricature is a kind of drawing in which there is a ludicrous exaggeration of certain outstanding features.

Left: This famous Greek statue called "The Victory of Samothrace"
is an excellent example of beautiful rhythmic line.
Right: "Mask of Anna Pavlowa," by Malvina Hoffman.

Rhythmic Lines in Face and Figure

Can you see rhythmic lines in arms, and legs, and heads, and bodies? The sculptor who made the great statue "Victory of Samothrace" could see and enjoy beautiful rhythms in the lines of the human body, above, L. The ancient Greeks used a single female figure with wings to symbolize victory. The "Victory of Samothrace" probably was meant to commemorate a great naval victory. There are no historical records to tell us exactly why the statue was made or what happened to it since the time of the ancient Greeks. The head and arms have been broken off and lost forever. Probably the hands held a trumpet upon which the Victory played the song of triumph. The pedestal was shaped like the prow of a boat. Can you see this great figure with sweeping wings standing as though it faced the wind as the boat cut through the water? Even without the head and arms it is exciting to behold. The swinging lines of the draperies and the strong lines of the body and wings create beautiful rhythmic patterns.

116

Lay tracing paper over the Victory figure and trace six lines which you think are most important in creating the strong rhythmic effect.

There is another splendid example of rhythmic-line pattern in the "Mask of Anna Pavlowa" by the great American woman sculptor Malvina Hoffman, page 118. The mask is done in wax, which adds to the delicate quality of the work. Notice the fine curves in the arch of the eyebrows, the eyelids, the mouth, the nostrils and the contour of the whole face. The jeweled headdress and the necklace echo the lovely curves of the face. The rhythmic pattern in this head is not as exciting as that in the "Victory of Samothrace" but it is just as beautiful in another way.

The very old and famous picture shown on page 120 is another fine example of flowing, rhythmic line. It was painted by Sandro Botticelli, an Italian painter who lived during the period of history when Columbus discovered America. He completed this picture nearly twenty years before Columbus made his first voyage to America. You see, artists have understood the rhythmic beauty of the human figure for many centuries. It is called "Spring" and is a symbolic representation of the spring season. Slender, graceful figures in a forest glade celebrate the coming of the spring. It is fanciful and charming with its fairylike figures, flying cherub, and spring flowers.

A very fine example of beautiful line is found in the marble bust called "Maidenhood" by a modern American sculptor, George Gray Barnard, page 120. The sweep of the hair drawn back over the lovely head, the delicate profile, the tilt of the head, and the curves of the shoulders produce a lovely rhythmic contour.

Action Creates Strong Rhythmic Movement

We have seen that the lines in the human figure may be beautifully harmonious. When the body is thrown into action re-

Above: This famous painting called "Spring," by Botticelli, is a fine example of rhythmic pattern.

Below: A marble bust called "Maidenhood," by George Gray Barnard. It is a beautiful example of rhythmic form.

quired by running, jumping, diving, skating or throwing, the lines of movement are greatly emphasized. Artists know this and sometimes portray the human figure in a strong action pose. One of the most famous statues in the world, made by the ancient Greek sculptor, Myron, shows an athlete in full action as he hurls the discus, page 122. The discus is the heavy plate which he holds in his right hand. He whirls about to gain force before making the throw. Myron caught the action of the figure just before the arm swings forward. The figure is full of strong, rhythmic movement. Note the beautiful swing of the line from the right hand down over the shoulders, down the left arm, and on down the bent leg. Then notice the beautiful, strong line starting at the head and sweeping down the right side of the body and right leg. The statue is exciting and dramatic.

There are many athletic activities in which the body creates fine, rhythmic movements. As we watch swimmers, runners, or skaters, we see these beautiful movements come and go. When the artist captures these movements in stone or paint, he gives us a kind of beauty that everyone enjoys. Running is especially concerned with swift movement. Artists have frequently chosen a runner for a subject, for this very reason.

Fine Proportions in the Human Figure

We are so familiar with the general appearance of the human figure that we do not always realize how beautiful it is in proportion. The sculptor must know all about proportions in the human figure if he is to produce good statues. He knows the proportions of all the parts in relation to others, such as the height in relation to the length of the head and the thickness and width of the chest, waist, and hips. Generally he tries to create a statue that is ideal in proportions. Many art authorities feel that the

COURTESY, DEPARTMENT OF FINE ARTS, CARNEGIE INSTITUTE

"The Discus Thrower," made by the Greek sculptor, Myron,
more than 2,000 years ago.

sculptors of ancient Greece were most successful in creating human
figures with beautiful and ideal proportions. Certainly the figure
of "The Discus Thrower" on this page is splendid in its proportions. Another athlete statue from ancient Greece is "The

Scraper" by Lysippus (Lī-sĭp'pŭs), page 124. Here again you will see a beautifully proportioned human figure. It is an ideal athlete's figure. The pose of the figure is hard to understand unless one knows something about the customs of Greek athletes. In his left hand the athlete holds a small stick or "strigil" with which he is gently scraping his skin. It was the custom for the Greek athlete to rub down with olive oil before exercise. This was to keep the skin and muscles in good condition. This left their skins very slippery. If they were playing a game in which they caught hold of each other, the oily skins would make it difficult. Can you imagine two such wrestlers trying to keep their holds? During exercise in the outdoor gymnasium, the oily skins would pick up a great deal of dust and dirt. Before bathing, the athletes would take their scrapers and remove all the oil and dirt that could be scraped off.

Do you notice the tree trunk close behind "The Scraper's" right leg? The sculptor used this device to strengthen the statue—that is, to attach it more firmly to its pedestal. Such statues stood outdoors and in case of earthquakes or high winds might be upset. The ancient Greek sculptors often used tree stumps or similar objects in this way to support their statues.

One of the most important proportions which the artist must consider is the height of the figure in relation to the length of the head. The average man's figure is seven or seven-and-one-half heads high. This means that the length of the head from crown to chin is contained seven to seven and one half times in the height of the whole figure. If you measure the Indian statue on page 124, you will find that it is about seven heads high. This statue was made by the American sculptress, Malvina Hoffman, who also made the mask of Anna Pavlowa mentioned near the start of this chapter. It is meant to represent a typical Blackfoot

A Greek athlete statue called "The Scraper," by Lysippus.

A statue by Malvina Hoffman representing a Blackfoot Indian of the western plains.

Indian of the western plains, and stands in the Hall of Man in the Field Museum, Chicago.

Now measure "The Scraper" for height. You will find that it is nearly eight heads high. Remember that Greek sculptors tried to make their statues with ideal rather than realistic proportions. It often happened that a fine athlete was over-large in some part of his body. But a statue in his honor would show his figure in ideal proportions.

Portraits in Stone and Paint

What is the purpose of a good portrait? Does it show only how a person looks, or should it do something more?

A good portrait is a good likeness and much more. It shows character and personality, or in other words it tells what the person is like. A likeness shows whether you have a straight or turned-up nose, a square or pointed chin, and other things of this nature. But a real portrait tells something about what kind of a person you are: whether you are bold or timid, serious or gay, and other characteristics.

Let us examine a few of the famous portrait studies in sculpture and painting to see how much they tell about character and personality. "The Laughing Cavalier," page 126, by Franz Hals shows us a gentleman of the seventeenth century dressed in his Sunday-best costume. We feel that he must be a bit vain because he chooses to wear such fancy clothes. He is gay and bold and dashing. Without a doubt he enjoys life greatly.

Now for similar personalities as revealed in portraits, look at the painting on page 127. It was painted about 350 years ago by a Japanese artist named Kiyomasu I. This is an ink and paint portrait of a famous actor in Japan at that time. He is dressed here as a gay young man about town. His coat is elaborately decorated with calligraphic symbols, which can be translated into phrases like "white waves," "storm," "flower," and others. These might have been words from a song or popular story. We can see that this fellow was very proud of his beautifully decorated clothes, and he swaggered just a little as he walked along. The Japanese actor and the cavalier were dashing gentlemen of their time.

It is great fun to read character from portraits. Try it with the portrait shown on page 128. It is a very famous statue of Abraham Lincoln by Augustus Saint-Gaudens, located in Lincoln Park,

*"The Laughing Cavalier," by Franz Hals. This portrait
study shows character and personality.*

Chicago. Of course, you already know something about the life
and character of Lincoln, but try to see what Saint-Gaudens has
told about the man in this great portrait statue.

Let each member of the class write down what he sees of personality in
the statue. Then compare answers.

日本嬋娟畫鳥居氏清倍圖

COURTESY, ART INSTITUTE OF CHICAGO

*An ink and paint portrait of a gay young Japanese man-about-town,
dressed in traditional costume.*

"Lincoln" by Augustus Saint-Gaudens. This statue stands at the south entrance to Lincoln Park in Chicago.

The quaint-looking wood statue you see here is a carved house post from New Zealand. It was made by the Maoris, who are the native inhabitants of this island country in the South Pacific. The flat head and strong legs suggest that this sturdy-looking young fellow might have held up a great amount of weight. The fierce countenance and decorations on the figure may be those of a warrior. This could be a warning to possible trespassers to stay away. One might suppose that the owner carved this statue to look like himself, or at least the way he wished to look to others! Every man thought of himself in a different way, so each house would display a different form of figure. A stranger might identify an occupant by studying the carvings for tribal rank or decorations. Judging from the house post illustrated here, this remarkable race of people developed a high degree of skill in decorative carving.

COURTESY, ART INSTITUTE OF CHICAGO

A Maori house post of the 18th century. This is a self-portrait of a fierce warrior.

Cartoons and Funny Pictures

You have seen figures and faces depicted in paintings and statues. Many of these examples were famous. At the beginning of the chapter we stated that we would look at cartoons, and see how they represent the human form. But the cartoon does more than that. It also shows us how people feel! Most cartoons are drawings of funny things that happen to people—like you and me.

Nearly everyone likes the "funnies." We all like to laugh, and funny pictures can give us many chuckles. In this chapter we'll learn a little about what it is that makes them amusing.

There is a great deal of cartoon drawing in our modern world. Practically every newspaper and many magazines give space to the funny pictures. Some magazines use cartoon drawings on their covers. Some advertisers use cartoons in their advertisements. Cartoons appear frequently on the moving-picture screen. However, funny pictures are not new in the twentieth century. Cartoons have been found on the walls of the Pharaohs' tombs in Egypt and on the walls of Roman buildings. But never in all history has there been so much cartoon drawing. If you like to read the "funnies" in the Sunday comic supplement, you can be glad that you did not live one hundred years ago.

Since there is so much comic drawing in our world, we should learn to appreciate the best of it. In this chapter we shall study some different types of funny pictures and try to find out what makes a cartoon or caricature amusing.

Clever Caricatures Are Amusing

Caricatures and cartoons alike exaggerate certain outstanding characteristics, but the caricature usually depicts someone real. On the other hand, the cartoon represents an idea.

Caricatures are really character studies.   A clever artist cannot
only amuse us by exaggerating certain characteristics but also
show us something about character and personality.   Peggy Bacon,
an American artist, is very good at this kind of caricature.   Her
picture, below, includes caricatures of several people.   The scene
is laid in an art gallery where a lecturer is explaining the beauty
of a picture to a group of tourists.   He looks more as though he
belongs at the sideshow in a circus than in an art gallery.   He is
not having a tremendous amount of success with his audience.
Peggy Bacon's caricatures here show us exactly how each person
reacts to his speech about the picture.

Which person is bored and skeptical?   Which one is checking up to
see if he is telling the truth?   Which one is so tired she can not take
another step?   Which ones are most impressed but do not really
understand what he is talking about?

"Esthetic Pleasure," by Peggy Bacon, a caricature of people
in an art gallery.

COURTESY, ASSOCIATED AMERICAN ARTISTS, INC.

Some Cartoons Are "Joke Drawings"

Another type of funny picture is the cartoon in which there is a joke. There are many kinds of joke cartoons, just as there are many kinds of jokes. For instance, we laugh at something ridiculous and quite impossible, at something which is a predicament to others, something very *unexpected,* or something very exasperating to those involved but laughable to those who look on.

The card pictured at the top of page 133 is a good example of the impossible, or unexpected. Perhaps the artist himself has spent some time in the hospital, and has felt just this way! He hasn't missed a detail. The bottles of pills, medicines, drops, and lotions are all there by the bed. The hot water bottle is ready, too, just in case! To complete the picture, the patient has a large box of chocolates and a book. This could be a real situation except for the fact that the cartoonist has substituted the large dog for the patient. Of course it's ridiculous! But that's what makes it amusing. And don't miss his lonely friend or relative waiting for him to come home. Doesn't he look pathetic?

In the cartoon at the lower left, the joke is on the mother because she is so baffled by her daughter's interest in food, but lack of interest in preparing it. Does this happen at your house?

The fourth cartoon amuses us because the man has solved his problem in such a very unusual and unexpected way. Clever drawing expresses the amazement of the visitor at the collection of musical instruments which are decorations for the living room.

Cheer Up!

Comic cartoons cheer us up because they are pictures of the funny side of our lives. Some examples of how they can cheer us are the get-well cards we've looked at, both here and in Chapter 6. The Dad's Day greeting was amusing, too, for its novelty.

HALLMARK CARDS, INC.

Above: Get-well cards with impossible situations.
Below: Cartoons based on real-life situations.

"I can't understand why anyone who is as interested in food as you are doesn't want to learn to cook!"

"I don't play any of them. Over a period of years I've bought them from the kid next door."

THE SATURDAY EVENING POST

AMERICAN MAGAZINE BY HARRY MACE   THE SATURDAY EVENING POST

Cartoons are often used to make light of things that are serious, or things that can be very troublesome in real life. A favorite trick of cartoonists is to find one small incident in real life and build a picture story around it. They have great fun during elections, at which time they poke fun at one candidate and then another. Also, they use incidents based on home life. These are popular because we all like to laugh at one another. Maybe the cartoonist is drawing you, or perhaps me! Has your mother ever scolded you for using a clean towel when your hands aren't clean, or for soiling the kitchen floor? Whitney Darrow has made such

COURTESY, SIMONI.

NOT <u>THE</u> MAD BOMBER !?!

an incident seem very funny. That is, you and I think it's funny.
Mother may not appreciate the joke as much, particularly if this
happened just after she cleaned the floor. Not many years ago
you might have found yourself in this very picture. Has the
cartoonist caught the lively mood of the two little cowboys? How
will this "sad" story end?

The cartoon above demonstrates how a cartoonist exaggerates

certain features and outstanding characteristics in a rather wild way. This cartoon makes fun of our desire to know important people. Compare the fussy, overdressed matron with the low-life, ragged character in his stove-pipe hat. The woman is exclaiming, "Not THE mad bomber?!" because she has read of him in the papers. She is obviously thrilled. The cartoonist drew this picture to make people laugh, yet there is a true basis for the idea.

Sometimes cartoons are drawn to illustrate current events, or to influence public opinion. These are called editorial cartoons. Many newspapers print an editorial cartoon regularly.

Ideas Are Important

A joke drawing is not a success unless the idea back of it is really clever. No matter how good the drawing, the cartoon without a good idea is a failure. Cartoonists spend a great deal of time getting ideas. They have to watch what is going on in the world about them so they can make jokes about it. As you have seen they may use very ordinary and everyday activities in their jokes.

Can you think of any clever ideas for cartoons? Try to find something in your own community for a joke drawing. Remember there are different ways of treating your idea.

1. Use symbolic figures.
2. Create an impossible, fantastic situation.
3. Create an absurd situation.
4. Show a catastrophe or accident to someone.

Be prepared to explain your idea to the class.

It is said that a good cartoon can express an idea more clearly and forcefully than ten times the amount of space in written words. Would you not rather look at a clever cartoon than read a column of words?

Comic Strips Are Popular

Practically every American boy and girl is familiar with the comic strips in the Sunday comic supplements of the newspapers. Probably you have favorite comic strips in your own newspaper. There are as many different types of comic strips as there are of "one spot" cartoons. Some of them are funny because the characters do impossible things; some are funny because the characters meet with various catastrophes; some are amusing because the characters say witty things; and some are amusing because the characters are so ridiculous. However, some so-called comic strips are not comic at all. They are adventure stories, detective stories, or romances.

List the comic strips read by members of the class. Try and classify them according to the following:
1. impossible situations
2. ridiculous and absurd situations
3. adventure story
4. love story
5. everyday situations which are amusing

Funny Pictures That Move

Everyone who watches television or goes to the movies is acquainted with funny pictures that move. Popeye, Tom Terrific, Bugs Bunny, Huckleberry Hound, Woody Woodpecker, and other amusing characters become very real and familiar to us. Have you noticed the way the newer characters are drawn? They are simpler, less "real," yet just as effective, aren't they? Famous tales such as *Snow White* have been animated in such a real manner that we are transferred to the land of make-believe.

The animation of drawings—which means adding motion to them—is one of the great developments in picture history. Animated cartoons made possible all sorts of amusing and fantastic

*The painting by Louise Pershing called "Dear Mrs. Smythe
Has Been Very Ill."*

effects which could not be produced in any other way. Rabbits
can throw elephants over a mountain range or uproot giant oak
trees with the greatest of ease, flowers can bloom and wither in
the period of a minute or two, fish can breathe out of water or
turtles can fly through the air, if the cartoonist so desires. Anything can happen. Color, music, and speech help make the
cartoon amusing and delightful. Many of the effects are breath-
takingly dramatic and beautiful, especially in full color.

Any feature-length animated cartoon requires thousands of
separate drawings, photographed and arranged on a strip of film
in successive order. When they are projected upon the screen,
we see the drawings in such rapid succession that the characters
appear to move their arms, legs, head, and bodies—an animated
cartoon.

Caricature in Painting

In order to express their ideas forcefully, by emphasizing or exaggerating certain features of a person or scene, some painters use caricature.　On page 136, an extremely blank-faced woman is calling on her friend who has been ill.　The cartoon reveals a personality of a very unpromising type, not likely to contribute anything toward making "poor Mrs. Smythe" feel better!　Note that the cookies seem ready to slide off the dish, and ask yourself whether this woman is going to bring much cheer and inspiration into the house!　"The Senate," below, is a striking example of caricature in a painting.　The Senator, a very ordinary looking man, is not getting much of a hearing in the nearly empty senate chamber.　This picture says sarcastic things about our senate. We call this kind of art social satire.

"The Senate," by William Gropper.

COURTESY, MUSEUM OF MODERN ART

"The Sewing Machine" by Hann Trier, a German artist.

A Fun Picture—but Meaningful

Are you surprised to find the picture of a sewing machine in a chapter called "Figures and Faces"? You probably did not know it was a sewing machine until you read the title. Certainly Hann Trier did not paint a realistic sewing machine. Instead he did something much more interesting and amusing.

This sewing machine is going full speed, the wheel is whirring, the needle is chattering, the white thread is jerking, and the action is exciting. Look at the picture and try to imagine that you are stitching as fast as you can make the machine go. What would be your reaction to the machine at such a time?

Hann Trier was really painting a state of mind—the personal feelings of the machine operator. He secured his effect with a clever caricature treatment of the sewing machine.

A

B

FIGURE 77. Caricatures in wood carving. A. Amusing caricature of cowboys roping their horses, by E. B. Quigley. B. Pleasing interpretation of Mother Goose figures, by Rudolf Mafko.

Caricatures in Wood

Amusing effects can be produced with wood as well as with paint or pen. The wood carvings in Figure 77 A show some cowboys roping their horses. The figures are made clever and amusing through emphasis of certain lines and proportions. The heads of the men and the feet of the horses are especially exaggerated. The group of wood carvings in Figure 77 B is delightful. Here are "Little Miss Muffet," "Bo-peep," "Old King Cole," "Mistress Mary," and "Little Boy Blue," carved from mahogany with silver accessories. Can you imagine a more charming group of decorative figures, so familiar to everyone yet carved with such freshness and appealing quality?

139

EXPERIENCES IN APPRECIATION

1. Collect pictures of the human figure in action. Make tracings which show the main lines of action. Is the movement rhythmic and smooth, or awkward? Explain.

2. Collect pictures of the human figure which show good proportions. Your collection should include newspaper pictures of champion athletes. Do you find any of these whose one part of the body seems overdeveloped? If so, how does it affect the beauty and harmony of the figure?

3. Make a study of the Greek-athlete statues and report to the class. Use pictures to tell the story of each statue. Be sure to point out the beauty of each figure.

4. Try reading character from portrait studies. Select paintings or statues that are known as good character studies.

5. What type of beauty in the human figure do you enjoy most? Does it prevent you from enjoying other types?

6. Study fashion drawings for proportions in the figure. How many heads high are they made?

7. Make a collection of caricatures. Study each one to see what features were exaggerated.

CREATIVE ACTIVITIES

1. Make sketches of the human figure standing, sitting, or lying down. Select poses which reveal nice, rhythmic lines.

2. Make an illustration showing a scene which you know. Use colored crayons, chalks, or poster paints. Show at least five people in your picture. Your subject might be "At the Football Game," "The Family Watches Television," or "In the Library."

3. Try doing a portrait study of someone you know. Work for a likeness but accent the lines and contours which will portray character.

4. Try to create a figure that is really comic.

5. Try a joke drawing.

6. Try to cartoon some local happening.

7. Try a painting in a caricature style. (See paintings on pages 139 and 140.) Your subject might be "In the School Cafeteria," "The Track Meet," "Sunday Picnic," or "The Dog Show."

8

BEAUTY IN FAMOUS SCULPTURE

T HERE IS a great deal of sculpture in the world. In every land people have modeled in clay and carved from stone and wood. Sometimes they have made tiny statuettes and sometimes colossal figures that amaze us with their size. Sculpture has been created for many reasons, sometimes because of a religious motive, sometimes as a memorial to an important person or for a particular occasion, sometimes to decorate a building, and sometimes for the fun of creating a beautiful effect. Certainly it would not be possible for us to learn about all the statues that were ever made. It is not even possible in this chapter to learn about all the important and famous sculpture in the world today. But we can make a beginning by getting acquainted with a few, well-known pieces of sculpture which many people have learned to know and enjoy. Some of these were made centuries ago and have been famous through past ages of history. Others were created in modern times and have also become famous.

In this study we are not concerned so much with *when* a statue was made as *why* it was made, *what is its meaning,* and *how to see its beauty.*

Several famous pieces of sculpture are discussed in the following pages. As you read about each piece try to answer these two questions:

1. What idea was the sculptor trying to express?
2. How did he manage to express his idea beautifully?

What is the appeal of the sculpture? What kind of beauty does it have?

Some Famous Memorial Sculptures

Already you have become acquainted with a very famous memorial statue, the Abraham Lincoln by Augustus Saint-Gaudens, which stands at the entrance to Lincoln Park in Chicago. See Figure 64. You will be interested to know that another of these statues stands in London, England. Bronze statues are first modeled in clay and then cast in the metal. Frequently more than one copy is made and thus we can have identical statues located in different places.

Everyone knows that Abraham Lincoln was a great president who was kind and just, a man with far-seeing vision who believed in equal rights for all men. He cared more for the welfare and happiness of the American people than for his own personal life. The sculptor, Saint-Gaudens, showed some of these characteristics in his statue. Lincoln stands with his head slightly bowed, his face serious and sad. His clothing is wrinkled and almost untidy. Behind him is the chair that symbolizes the presidency of the United States of America. But it is not the chair which gives the statue its great dignity and majesty. It is the figure itself, tall, gaunt, and powerful, which is so impressive. Lincoln might have looked so when he delivered his great speech at Gettysburg.

Another famous statue of Lincoln is that by the American sculptor Daniel Chester French. The statue, Figure 78, is placed in the Lincoln Memorial, Washington, D. C. This, too, is a tremendously impressive statue. The great, seated figure seems to look out across our country through time and foresee what its future holds.

PHOTOGRAPH BY EWING GALLOWAY, NEW YORK

FIGURE 78. Dramatic night view of Daniel Chester French's statue of Abraham Lincoln, located in the Lincoln Memorial, Washington, D. C.

Compare the statues of Lincoln by French and Saint-Gaudens. This does not mean that you have to try to say that one is better than the other. You may prefer one but like the other also. Try to put into words the qualities which are most marked in each statue. Look for fine rhythms, interesting proportions, emphasis, and balance.

Many thousands of people have seen each of these statues. If you chance to be one of them, describe your visit and your impressions.

The Mount Rushmore National Memorial, located in the Black

FIGURE 79. Mount Rushmore National Memorial, South Dakota, by the famous American sculptor, Gutzon Borglum.

Hills, South Dakota, is a memorial to four great American presidents by the American sculptor, Gutzon Borglum. The colossal heads of Washington, Jefferson, Theodore Roosevelt, and Lincoln were sculptured in the rock of the mountainside. The picture in Figure 79 does not give an impression of their immense size. Each face from the chin to the top of the head measures about sixty feet.

The idea for this memorial to these four great men was conceived by the sculptor and he was finally commissioned by the federal government to undertake the sculpture. It was a huge engineering job to cut these enormous heads from the face of the mountain, and required many years to complete it.

History tells us that these men, George Washington, Thomas Jefferson, Theodore Roosevelt, and Abraham Lincoln had much to do with the foundation upon which our government was built. The impressive memorial carved on the weather beaten rock of Mount Rushmore serves to remind us of their wisdom in the troubled times of the past.

Can you quote a line of wisdom from each of the four presidents? If need be, consult your history books.

The memorial sculptures just discussed were erected in honor of persons whose names we know and respect. Sometimes a memorial sculpture is erected in honor of people whose names we may not know but whose deeds we do know and admire. A statue called "The Pioneer Woman," Figure 80, has been erected in Ponca City, Oklahoma, in honor of the pioneer mothers. Women who joined the pioneer movement in the early days of our country were brave and strong. They rode in covered wagons on rough trails; they suffered the hardships of life in the wilderness; they raised their children without the help of doctors, schools, or churches. This was a great achievement. In "The Pioneer Woman" the sculptor, Bryant Baker, has expressed the courage and strength of these women who helped to settle our western states. The mother strides forward grasping her son by the hand and carrying her Bible and a bundle of treasured possessions in the other arm.

Famous Tomb Sculpture

Since the earliest days of civilization sculpture has been used to decorate the tombs of those who have died. The cemeteries of today contain many sculptured pieces which mark the graves.

FIGURE 80. "The Pioneer Woman," by Bryant Baker. Located in
Ponca City, Okla.

146

Some tomb sculptures both of past and present times have become famous because of their beauty and meaning.

Five thousand years ago in Egypt the great pharaoh Khephren (pronounced Kĕf'-ren) or Khafra (pronounced Kä'-frà) built one of the great pyramids for his tomb. It took thousands of men many years to build this gigantic stone structure. It is as tall at the peak as a thirty-five story sky-scraper and spreads out over thirteen acres of ground. Why did Khephren want such an enormous tomb? Partly to tell the world what a great and mighty king he was, but more especially because of what the Egyptians at that time believed about life after death.

They believed that when a person died, a spirit separated from the body at the moment of death. This spirit was invisible and was called a Ka (pronounced kä). For a time the Ka might live in one's own house but one would not know it because a Ka was invisible. It might live for a time in the body of a cat or beetle. No one ever harmed a cat or a beetle because if he did he might injure the Ka of someone he had known. Finally the Ka was supposed to wander off into some distant place, a Spirit World, and stay for hundreds, thousands, even hundreds of thousands of years. But at some time it would return. When it came back it would look for its own tomb and its own body. If the tomb had not been entered by any living being and the body had not been disturbed, then the Ka could re-enter its own body and would live eternally.

Naturally the Egyptian pharoah wished to enjoy eternal life. Therefore he would build himself as strong a tomb as possible in which he would live forever. Khephren was a rich and powerful king who could afford to build a giant pyramid for his tomb.

In Figure 81 you can see the buildings which belonged to Khephren's pyramid. Close to the stone wall surrounding the

FIGURE 81. A sketch which shows how Khephren's pyramid, chapel, causeway, and temple may have looked 5,000 years ago.

pyramid is a chapel. This chapel is not an entrance to the pyramid but merely stands beside it. From the chapel, a long covered passageway, called a causeway, leads down over the sand hills and cliffs to the valley of the Nile. At the end is another building which was built as a vestibule or entrance and is known as the Valley Temple. Khephren had several statues of himself placed in this Valley Temple. Probably he expected them to serve him after he was dead and buried. Perhaps they were sentinels who guarded his tomb eternally. Very likely they were also expected to serve as watchers for his Ka when it wandered back from the Spirit World. Or they would help the Ka to find its own body so Khephren would live forever! To us these things seem strange, but we live now in the twentieth century. No one now believes that there is a Ka which will re-enter its own body and bring eternal life. However, it is interesting to study the beliefs and customs of the Egyptian people who lived long ago. It explains for us why Khephren's pyramid was so huge and why his statues stood in the Valley Temple.

When Khephren was buried his people took good care of his pyramid and the other buildings. Every day some of them entered the dark, gloomy Valley Temple, passed the great statues, climbed the long covered passageway to the chapel, and there left fresh food. They believed that Khephren's Ka might return any moment and when it did there must be fresh food ready for it. But five thousand years is a very long time. After awhile there were other kings and other things to think about. The pyramid and buildings were left alone and neglected. The winds of the desert blew and the sands shifted. Finally, the chapel, the passageway, and the temple were entirely covered over. As time went on people forgot that there were any buildings at all near the pyramid. Not till modern times did archaeologists dig in the sands around the pyramid and find the ruins of the chapel, the passageway, and the temple.

Sand is heavy and, as you may guess, the buildings had caved in. All the statues but one in the Valley Temple were broken to bits. You can see some broken places in the remaining Khephren statue, Figure 82. The original of the statue stands in the museum at Cairo today.

Notice that the end of the beard is broken off. Every Egyptian king had to wear a beard because it was a sign of power, strength, and wisdom. It became the custom for the king sometimes to wear a false beard which he put on just as another king might wear a crown. Khephren's beard rather looks as though it were his own but in some of the Egyptian statues you can see the straps which hold the beard to the headdress. The headdress was made from a piece of very stiff linen cloth, though it looks in the statue as if it were made from some thick, heavy material.

The design on the side of Khephren's chair is hieroglyphic writing. Hieroglyphs are a kind of picture writing. In the upper part of the design is the lotus flower which stands for the Upper Kingdom or the part of Egypt around the upper part of the river. In the lower part of the design is the papyrus which stands for the Lower Kingdom or the part of the country around the delta and mouth of the river. The lines from the lotus and from the papyrus are joined together in a knot. This means that the two kingdoms were joined together under the rule of Khephren.

Notice how stiff and straight and motionless is the figure of Khephren. He seems to have sat for centuries waiting for his Ka. Something about the statue seems to suggest eternity itself. There is no delicacy or liveliness about it. Instead it is powerful, dignified, majestic. Khephren is every bit a king.

The early Egyptian sculptors never cut out any open places in their statues. You will see that in the Khephren statue there are no open places under the chair, between the legs, or around the linen headdress. The sculpture is left in one solid piece. It has been suggested that perhaps the stone was too hard and their tools too crude to encourage any extra cutting. Probably this was not the reason. More likely they preferred the heavy, massive effect produced by their solid statues. Perhaps they felt that the statues would endure longer if they were made as strong and solid as possible.

Some three thousand years after the Khephren statues were made for his pyramid tomb, the ancient Greeks made some beautiful tomb sculptures to mark the graves of their dead. The slab shown in Figure 83 was discovered in a cemetery near Athens. It remains in its original position after more than two thousand years.

The Monument of Hegeso, Figure 83, was intended as a grave memorial for a woman of Athens. The lady is shown sitting in her chair and holding in her hands a jewelled ornament or trinket, possibly a string of beads. The object itself has long since been lost but we can see from the position of her hands what she was doing. Her maidservant stands before her holding a jewel box from which she took the trinket. This little scene might have

FIGURE 82. *Khephren, a pyramid statue made 5,000 years ago in Egypt.*
FIGURE 83. *The Monument of Hegeso, a tomb memorial from ancient Greece.*

been an incident in her everyday life. It was customary among the Greeks to use such incidents in their grave memorials.

Now think of the Hegeso Monument from the art standpoint. It is a beautifully designed panel. The main lines of the seated figure echo the rectangular shape of the rectangle, but with delightful variations. The curves in the back and legs of the chair are strong and fine. They are repeated in the smaller, more delicate curves of the draperies. Notice, too, the strong vertical lines in parts of the drapery. The figure of the maidservant strengthens the left-hand side of the design and at the same time adds a delightful rhythm of lines and forms.

> Lay tracing paper over the picture in Figure 83 and trace the twelve lines which seems to you most important in producing the rhythmic pattern.

This kind of sculpture in the Monument of Hegeso is called bas-relief (*bas* pronounced to rhyme with *ma* with no *s* sound). The effect is secured by carving the background away from the subject. You will find that a great deal of this kind of sculpture is used today in the decoration of buildings.

Since the time of the ancient Greeks, sculpture has been used in every period of history to decorate tombs. In our own cemeteries we have statues and bas-reliefs of various kinds. Probably you are familiar with some in your own community.

Sculpture for Architectural Decoration and Other Purposes

For many centuries sculpture has been used to decorate buildings. From ancient times down to the twentieth century both interiors and exteriors of temples, churches, and public buildings have been ornamented with statues and bas-reliefs.

The two bas-relief sculptures in Figure 84 decorate the exterior of the building of the Buhl Planetarium and Institute of Popular Science in Pittsburgh, Pennsylvania. Sidney Waugh, an American, is the sculptor. In these two sculptures he has achieved an effect of great power and vitality. In the slab called "The Heavens" we feel that here is a force dynamic and supreme beyond all others. In "The Earth" we also feel force and power, though perhaps more controlled, the control that man has achieved over the elements of the world.

> Discuss the sculpture used for architectural decoration in your own community.

Sculpture used for architectural decoration in another age is shown in Figure 85. Here is the doorway of an old cathedral built in the thirteenth century in Bordeaux, France. The figure representing Pope Clement V stands in a dominating position before the central column. On either side are the figures of bishops. Just above the doorway is a row of figures at a table, depicting "The Last Supper." In the second row of figures above

FIGURE 84.   Two sculpture decorations by Sidney Waugh on the Buhl Planetarium and Institute of Popular Science.

the doorway is "The Ascension." In the point of the arch
Christ sits on his throne in Heaven with an angel standing
on either side. Then kneeling angels just fill the remaining
end spaces. This was a nice problem in the space filling for the
sculptor. In the channels of the great, pointed arch smaller figures of the saints, disciples, and prophets enhance the form of
the arch. Notice how every bit of the decoration conforms to the
general shape of the doorway. Good decoration always echoes
and enhances the structural form.

Sometimes sculpture is created for the purpose of civic decoration. The city authorities commission a sculptor to create a work
which will beautify a park or other public spot. Of course, such
a sculpture may also be a memorial to a person or past event, as
in the case of the Columbus Memorial in Washington. Another
work by the same sculptor, Lorado Taft, is the Great Lakes Fountain in Chicago. This fountain, Figure 86, is a feature in the
City Beautiful Plan. Sculptor Taft took as his theme the Great
Lakes, which are important to Chicago. From your study of geog-
raphy you probably have learned that Chicago grew to be a great
city partly because of its position on Lake Michigan. The uppermost figure in the fountain represents Lake Superior; immediately
below is Huron. Michigan to the left pours her waters into
Huron's basin. From Huron the water falls into Erie's shell, then
into Ontario's, and away to the ocean. The fountain is beautifully designed. The forms are graceful yet strong. Each figure
is interesting and yet the whole group is unified and pleasing.
Can you trace the main rhythmic movement in the fountain?

What sculptures are there in your community which you think add to
the beauty of the city? Why was each piece erected? What is the idea
the sculptor was trying to express? How well do you think he managed it?

FIGURE 85. A doorway from the Gothic cathedral in Bordeaux, France, having fine sculpture decorations.

155

FIGURE 86. "The Fountain of the Great Lakes" by Lorado Taft.

156

There are many uses for sculpture other than those which we have already discussed. Often it has been used for religious purposes to decorate altars, shrines, and churches. Sometimes the chief aim of a statue is a portrait. Thousands of portrait figures and busts have been made. Instead of going to a photographer or portrait painter, people who can afford it sometimes go to a sculptor and ask him to do their portraits. Sometimes sculpture is created merely because the sculptor wants to create a thing of beauty. He has an idea which he expresses in clay, bronze, or marble. He may have no idea how the sculpture will be used, if at all. He simply produces a fine piece of work. We enjoy it because he expressed his theme beautifully. Such a piece of work is "The Sun Vow" by Hermon A. MacNeil, Figure 87. It was not meant as a memorial, monument, or architectural decoration, but merely as a fine, bronze sculpture. The old Indian watches while the Indian boy shoots his arrow straight into the sun. The boy is proving that he has become strong and skillful with his bow and arrow. We enjoy the fine modeling of the figures, the swing of the lines in the bow, the outstretched arm, and the young body. We also enjoy the way strength and dignity are expressed in the older figure.

Sculpture in Our Homes

We have been discussing famous statues located in parks, art galleries, and other public places. Certainly we can enjoy these works of art when we see them in their splendid settings. We can even enjoy pictures of them. But we can enjoy smaller sculptures every day if we plan to have them in our homes. Nearly everyone has a picture or two on his walls. For the price of a picture he might have a bas-relief carving on his wall or a small statue on his mantel. The horse sculptures in Chapter Two, Fig-

FIGURE 87. "The Sun Vow," by Hermon A. MacNeil.

ures 13 and 14, are suitable for home decoration. Many famous sculptures are reproduced in small sizes at moderate prices. The garden is another place where sculpture is most desirable. Nymphs, birds, little child figures among the flowers and at the garden pool add decorative touches to a garden.

> Do you know any home where a piece of sculpture adds to the attractiveness of the place? If you could choose one piece of sculpture for your own home, what would it be and where would you put it?

EXPERIENCES IN APPRECIATION

1. Make a list and collect pictures of the memorial sculpture with which you are acquainted. Be prepared to tell your class about at least two sculptures. Report on the person or event to which the memorials were erected. Explain how the sculptor expressed his idea and show how well he did it.

2. Select some past event in your own community which you think is worthy of a memorial sculpture. Try to create in your mind an idea for this memorial. This does not require ability to do sculpture but thinking and imagination.

3. What is your favorite piece of sculpture? Why?

4. Select a theme such as Indian sculpture. Collect information and pictures about your subject. Report to the class. Other themes which you might choose are Sculpture for Our Homes, Animal Sculpture, Greek Athlete Sculpture, or Greek Gods and Goddesses in Sculpture.

5. The largest statue in America is the Statue of Liberty. Learn the story of the statue, its meaning, and any other data about it. What do you think of it in terms of art quality, rhythmic movement, expressiveness, and sculptural quality? The sculptor was Frederic Auguste Bartholdi. An encyclopedia is a good source of information.

6. Most great sculptures are created first by means of clay modeling. Then the model is translated into stone or bronze. If possible arrange for a demonstration of molding from a clay model.

7. Survey your community with the idea that a statue can be erected for beautification. What do you think it should be? Where should it be placed?

8. Arrange a demonstration, perhaps for an auditorium program, by a local sculptor.

CREATIVE ACTIVITIES

1. Choose a subject for clay modeling which interests you. It should be something with which you are familiar, such as your pet dog or cat, your favorite animal in the zoo, a horse, the head of a friend, or your idea of Madonna and Child.

Before you begin modeling, think of the special characteristic which you wish to emphasize most. The figure should be at least 6 inches high.

When the modeling is partly completed, hold a class consultation on the success of the work. Be prepared to give suggestions to others and to receive them yourself. Remember that your piece should emphasize the characteristic which you selected. Continue to work for the best expression of it which you can make.

2. Choose a subject for a bas-relief in clay modeling. This should tell a story such as "The Westward Movement of the Pioneers." You might choose some historical incident in your locality.

Keep the composition of the bas-relief simple. It should be at least 10 inches by 5 inches.

3. Study the modeling in bas-relief on American coins. The designs on pennies, nickels, dimes, and other coins are interesting and many of them are beautiful. The buffalo nickel was designed by a famous artist, James Earle Fraser, and is considered interesting and beautiful.

Make your own design for the nickel of the future. Think of a subject which is suitable for an American coin. Use a circle at least three inches in diameter and keep the design simple enough so that it could be reduced to the size of a nickel without being crowded. After you have perfected your design on paper, work it out in clay. Keep it the same size, 3 inches in diameter.

9

FINE PAINTINGS TO REMEMBER

MOST OF US cannot afford to buy all the fine pictures that we should like to own. However, the lack of money need not prevent us from becoming acquainted with the world's greatest paintings. We can learn to know and enjoy them even though we cannot own them. Anyone can stand before a beautiful picture in an art gallery and enjoy it just as much as the man who can write a check and take it home with him. Of course, the man who has a private art gallery can look at his pictures often and enjoy their beauty, but the rest of us can enjoy our memories of the fine pictures that we have seen. Our own private art galleries are in our heads. They can bring us a great deal of satisfaction and pleasure. These mental picture galleries cost us nothing but the time spent in getting acquainted with the pictures.

A study of great paintings can be a lifetime work. For hundreds of years, artists have been painting fine pictures. Our private picture galleries can hold only a few of these thousands of paintings. We can not hope to become acquainted with a great number of pictures in one chapter. Fifteen paintings have been selected for you to add to your private collection. They have not been chosen because they are the most famous, or the most valuable, or the most beautiful, but because they are favorites with a great many boys and girls and therefore a part of the beauty to be found in their world.

Four Landscapes—All Different

There are many things to see in the great outdoors—trees, hills, mountains, valleys, clouds, rivers, and lakes. From all this, the landscape painter must choose the things that will go into his picture. He must decide also what effect or impression he wants in his painting. He may wish to have a pretty, peaceful little scene or perhaps a mighty and exciting effect. There are many different kinds of landscapes and we can enjoy each one for what it shows us.

FIGURE 88. "The Bridge of Trysts," by Corot.

OWNED BY ART INSTITUTE OF CHICAGO (POTTER PALMER COLLECTION

"The Bridge of Trysts," by Corot

The landscape in Figure 88 is a landscape in France. It was painted by Jean-Baptiste Camille Corot (Kō-rō′). Corot was born in 1796 and died in 1875. He painted landscapes with lovely, poetic effects. In this one we see talking and waiting figures at the place where lovers were said to meet. The figures, however, are not the most important part of the picture. Note the soft, lovely mass of foliage arched in the sky beyond the bridge, and the slender, graceful tree trunks at the left.

Corot spent a great deal of time outdoors with his sketchbook. He tramped the woods and the fields studying trees, skies, clouds, and streams. Many of his trips were early in the morning because he especially liked the misty, twilight effects which come just before daybreak. Because he carried his sketchbook and pencils with him, he was considered a little peculiar. One hundred years ago in France, artists did all their work in their studios. It was most unusual for an artist to do any drawing or painting outdoors where he could see the actual scene. In fact landscapes themselves were practically unknown in French art until the time of Corot. They had been used chiefly as backgrounds or settings for pictures with people as the chief interest. Portraits, religious themes, and Greek myths were subjects for paintings. Landscape alone had not been considered a worthy subject for a picture. Artists of other countries had painted landscapes but French artists up until this time had not wanted to devote their time to it. You can see why Corot was considered a queer artist, and why his work was not popular at the time. He did not sell a picture until he was nearly fifty years old. People did not want his pictures. However, he could spend his time at painting instead of earning a living because his father gave him a small allowance. When Corot was young his father had hoped he would go into the linen business with him but Corot wanted to paint. Finally his father allowed him to go to Italy and study. In later years Corot moved from Paris to the village of Barbizon, located near Fontainebleau Forest. There he discovered the loveliness of nature and put it into his paintings.

Several other artists, friends of Corot's, also lived at Barbizon and painted outdoors. This group of artists is known as the Barbizon school. We shall become acquainted with another of them later in this chapter.

In the later years of Corot's life his work became very popular and he sold a great many pictures at high price. The public had decided that, after all, landscapes could be beautiful pictures.

"Winter Sun," by Wendell Orosz

The picture at the top of the opposite page was painted by Wendell Orosz, a young American artist who has had no formal art training. His natural talent and feeling for art expression have brought him success.

"Winter Sun" won the William J. Strassburger Memorial Prize "For a Realistic Oil Painting" in the 1959 Bicentennial Exhibition of the Associate Artists of Pittsburgh.

"Winter Sun" is the kind of painting which helps us to see new kinds of beauty in nature that we would have missed if we had not seen the painting. First of all, our attention is caught by the lovely rhythmic pattern of the bare trees seen against the houses and hills. The vertical upward movement of the tree trunks, each with its particular manner of curving slightly to left and right, is interesting. The large branches swinging to the left help to create a fascinating design. Notice how the shadows of the branches on the snow echo the rhythmic movement toward the left. It seems as though the winds of winter must have swept

FIGURE 89. "Winter Sun" by Wendell Orosz.

the branches along their way, but we also feel the dynamic quality in the lines of growth as tree trunks and branches have thrust up.

The cold sunlight of winter sheds a pale radiance over all. The artist has woven it into the pattern of trees and houses.

Probably you will never see an actual scene like that in "Winter Sun," but you might see nature the way that Wendell Orosz would see it. The artist does not put all the details of nature into his picture. Instead he selects the features which are important in creating a beautiful effect. Perhaps you can think of details which the painter of "Winter Sun" omitted in order to create the effect that he desired.

165

FIGURE 90. *"Stone City, Iowa," by Grant Wood.*

"Stone City, Iowa," by Grant Wood

Grant Wood, a famous American artist, was known as a "regional painter," which means that he chose to paint pictures of people and places in his own part of the country—Iowa. He once studied in Paris, France, sometimes called the art center of the world. After a time, he said he thought there was plenty to paint in Iowa, so he went back home and remained there the rest of his life, painting pictures of people and things with which he was familiar. John Steuart Curry, who painted "The Tornado" (page 183) was another regional artist, painting life in Kansas.

In the painting above, Grant Wood chose as his subject a small town in his home state. He shows us a view of the town such as we might see from an airplane flying at low altitude. Grant Wood painted in his own individual way. Unlike Corot, Grant Wood made his picture into a kind of design or pattern. The cornfield is a pretty, little, allover decoration; the trees are toy trees; the houses are little boxes; and the hills are modeled as in a scene on a sand table. It is Grant Wood's way of portraying a scene in Iowa. We cannot help but like his way of showing us beauty in our country.

"America," by Rockwell Kent

Here is another modern landscape, Figure 91, but painted in an entirely different manner. Its name gives us a clue to its meaning. It symbolizes our great country and the pioneers who settled it. There is a wooded hilltop in the foreground, a vast expanse of plains beyond, and in the distance great mountains. Over it all the sun sheds a clear, strong light. The little log cabin in the near foreground stands for all the log cabins built by brave pioneers.

FIGURE 91. "America," by Rockwell Kent.

Near it a man chops wood, symbolizing what man has done in the struggle to settle this country, and on the other side of the cabin a woman hangs laundry on the line, symbolizing woman's share of work in the pioneer movement. The artist has expressed these ideas in his own style. Somehow he gives us a feeling of vast spaces, majestic heights, and never-ending skies.

Rockwell Kent also is a twentieth-century American artist. He has traveled and painted in Alaska, Greenland, and other out-of-the-way places. On his travels he has found ideas for his landscapes.

Towns and Cities—Three Pictures

There was a time when painters thought that a beautiful outdoors scene could be found only in the country. Then some of them found that there is beauty in towns and cities. Those who have the eye to see it can find beauty in buildings and bridges, city streets, factories, and village houses.

"End of the Day," by Burchfield

Would you think of looking for a beautiful picture in a village street of dingy houses? The American artist Charles Burchfield found one on a winter day in a mining town. He calls it "End of Day," Figure 92. Men are coming home from their work in the steel mills and daylight has begun to fade. The houses are old and ramshackle, but Burchfield has painted them with a rhythmic beauty. Notice that as you look into the picture you look *down* the street. It is a fine piece of perspective drawing. Perhaps you will say, "This is not a pretty picture." Perhaps it is not *pretty,* but it has a kind of somber beauty. Burchfield selects subjects for his paintings that are common, everyday scenes, and often they are ugly. But he paints them in such a way that they seem picturesque and sometimes romantic. Corot made his landscapes romantic and in a way Burchfield does the same thing with his ugly, village street. He is a poet in paint.

Do you know an ugly street and can you imagine how it would look if Burchfield painted it?

"Silver Light," by Jonas Lie

In this picture, Figure 93, of a harbor with boats and buildings, the artist had a still different aim. The name of the picture should give you a clue to his particular aim. It was not the buildings, nor the boats, nor the water, but the light falling upon the scene. Notice how beautifully it is reflected from the surface of the ruffled water. It is a charming study of reflected light and atmospheric effect.

FIGURE 92. "End of Day," by Charles Burchfield.

COURTESY, THE PENNSYLVANIA ACADEMY OF FINE ARTS

FIGURE 93. *"Silver Light," by Jonas Lie.*

Jonas Lie (Lee) was an American artist who painted many pictures of boats, water, houses, and trees. Always he tried to show how they looked under a special effect of sunlight and shadow.

"Steel, Steam, and Smoke," by Everett Warner

Some artists find beauty in the busy turmoil of a great industrial city. Everett Warner has shown us beauty in a view of Pittsburgh's steel mills. See Figure 94. In the foreground we see a small house and yard surrounded by a dilapidated fence. Across the river there are giant smokestacks which belch forth great clouds of smoke and steam. The plain little house is the center of interest and it is interesting to see how Warner managed to emphasize it. It is near the center of the canvas and its light color stands out against a darker background. The fence helps to set it forth and the roadway also emphasizes it. Altogether, the artist has created a picture with interesting composition. The lines and

170

forms are put together to make a good composition. You will be interested to know that he painted the scene as it really is and changed nothing. He searched the city until he found a spot where he could paint a picture as the scene really was, and at the same time have a pleasing composition. Of course, he emphasized certain things and subordinated others. He did not show every detail of the houses at the edges of the picture, nor did he make them stand out so distinctly as the house in the center. Although this picture is a truthful representation of the scene, it could never be mistaken for a photograph. It is obviously a painting. We can see how the artist used his brush, and how he blended his tones to emphasize the beauty of the scene.

FIGURE 94. "Steel, Steam, and Smoke," by Everett Warner.

Select a scene in your community which is generally thought of as lacking beauty. Can you see it as Everett Warner might have painted it? Even if you can not paint it to your own satisfaction, you can explain how you would plan the picture.

Portraits in Paint—Four Pictures

Pictures of people have been popular subjects for painting since its beginning. Some artists so like to paint portraits they confine themselves entirely to that kind of painting.

Each of the four portraits here tells its own story, and also shows what the artist was trying to express. Try answering the following questions to see if you can discover what each portrait expresses in Figures 95, 96, 97, and 98.

In which one do you think the artist was chiefly interested in creating an effect of lovely rhythmic line?

In which one did the artist show a person of stern, rough personality?

In which portrait does the person seem tired and discouraged?

In which one does the artist suggest that the people are wealthy and aristocratic?

Which one appeals most to you?

"Aurora Leigh," by John White Alexander

The portrait shown in Figure 95 is very charming. Alexander liked to create fine, decorative effects in his portraits. In this one the young lady's full skirt, the flowing sleeve, and the streamers from her hat combine to produce a lovely, rhythmic movement. The lines of the handsome, white collie blend beautifully into this rhythm. The young lady looks at us from under her big hat in a rather shy and gracious manner. Some people do not like this kind of portrait because the clothing is too important and too little attention is paid to the real person. Other people like that effect very much and do not mind the emphasis on costume.

John Alexander was born in Pittsburgh, Pennsylvania, where he worked as a boy in a telegraph station. One day when he was alone in the station, a man came in and wrote an important message to be sent. When the operator came back, he discovered that the man had forgotten to sign his name. The operator asked Alexander if he knew the man. Alexander replied, "No, but I can draw his picture." He drew the picture so well that the operator knew who had sent the message. This incident so interested an official of the company that he later helped Alexander to get his art training. Knowing this about Alexander's ability to draw faces, we can feel sure that Aurora's Leigh's portrait is a good likeness.

"The Castilian Shepherd," by Zuloaga

Here is a portrait, Figure 96, that is not like the one we have just studied. It is bolder and more exciting. The painting is more direct and more modern in treatment. The artist has paid some attention both to character in the man's face and to his clothing. We see at once that he is an outdoors man. His clothing is heavy and rough and his face is weather-beaten. Even without knowing the title we could guess that he is a shepherd because of his crook. Notice the rocky hilltop and the stormy sky. We know that his work often keeps him out in very bad weather. The Castilian shepherd is a man who cares for sheep in the mountainous region of Spain.

Three boys who were looking at this portrait were asked to read from the shepherd's face his character and personality. One of them said, "I think he would be mean. I'd hate to have him mad at me!" The second boy said, "But I think he looks kind." The third boy made both these ideas seem right when he said, "I think he would be goodnatured as long as things went right. But when things went wrong he would be tough about it." Perhaps this is the thing that Zuloaga was trying to express.

Zuloaga is a Spanish artist who is famous for his ability to paint character in a dramatic way.

Two Self-Portraits by Rembrandt

In Figures 97 and 98 you will see two portraits of the same man, both painted by himself. What can you read from these portraits about the man himself? Of course, you will see at once that in one portrait he is young and in the other he is old. What more can you discover in the faces?

FIGURE 95. "Aurora Leigh," by John White Alexander.
FIGURE 96. "The Castilian Shepherd," by Ignacio Zuloaga.

Write down everything you can see in each portrait. How did Rembrandt feel about himself and his life in each case? After you have done your best, read the following story.

Rembrandt Harmenszoon van Rijn lived three hundred years ago in Holland. His long name means that he was Rembrandt, son of Harmens of the Rhine. His father was a miller whose mill stood on the Rhine River. By the time Rembrandt was fifteen his father saw that his son was not much good at anything except art, so Rembrandt was apprenticed to an artist. As a young man Rembrandt moved to Amsterdam and soon became the leading artist in the city. His pictures were popular and he charged high prices. He married a beautiful girl named Saskia. He adored his Saskia and dressed her in silks and velvets, and adorned her with jewels. Naturally he painted many portraits of Saskia. He, too,

FIGURE 97. Rembrandt's self-portrait when he was a young man.
FIGURE 98. Rembrandt's self-portrait when he was an old man.

COURTESY, UNIVERSITY PRINTS   COURTESY, MR. H. E. TEN CATE,
                                                    ALMELO, HOLLAND

liked to dress in expensive clothing and show himself as a fine gentleman. He also bought many paintings and other works of art until his house became a museum. He and Saskia lived in a grand manner and spent a great deal of money. In spite of his many commissions and high prices, he spent more than he made.

His portrait of himself in Figure 97 was painted during this period of his life when he was popular and famous. You can see his fine clothes. You can see, too, that he was proud and perhaps a little vain. He was full of self-confidence and a trifle boastful.

Up to this time Rembrandt's life was a fine success story. Then when he was thirty-six years old came tragedy. Two catastrophes befell him: Saskia died; the public turned against his pictures.

It was the fashion in Rembrandt's time for groups of men such as the officers of a militia company or the heads of a business organization to commission a painter to do a group portrait of themselves. The officers of Captain Banning Cock's civic guards ordered a group portrait from Rembrandt. They expected to see themselves standing or sitting in a group around a table, each in an equally prominent position. Rembrandt painted a huge canvas showing the company as it sallied forth at noon on its way to do guard duty on the city walls. Naturally the first figures were in full sunlight, but others were caught in the shadow of the great gateway. The faces of a few men show clearly, but others are hidden by those in front and obscured by shadow. This did not please the officers at all, especially those in the background. There was a great row about it. Rembrandt refused to change it because he knew it was a good picture and that it would be ruined if every face and figure were equally prominent.

The picture was called "The Sortie of the Banning Cock Company." Sortie means a sudden sally into the open by a group of soldiers. The company would not hang the picture in the great room for which it was intended and put it into a small anteroom. In order to make it fit the wall space they cut off a strip at one side spoiling the balance and composition. Later it was hung in a room which was heated with a peat fire. The black smoke from the burning peat covered the picture with a layer of black soot. This so darkened the picture that people came to believe that it was meant for a night picture and called it "The Night Watch." That is the name by which it is most generally known today. Remember that it was really a picture at high noon with full sunlight! The picture now occupies a room to itself in the museum in Amsterdam.

After this time Rembrandt received very few commissions. His creditors forced him into bankruptcy. His house, his art collections, his own paintings, and even his clothing were sold for debt. He moved to a smaller, poorer house. His struggles with poverty were long and hard. However, he continued to paint. Sometimes he had difficulty in obtaining colors and canvas for his pictures but he managed to paint pictures. Perhaps for want of other subjects, he continued to paint self-portraits. That in Figure 98 was painted in 1662, a few years before his death. Here is a man who is sad and disillusioned. The world has treated him harshly, but he is patient and philosophical. It is hard to believe that this is the same man as the confident young fellow in the earlier portrait.

People at Play—One Picture

Some artists choose as subjects for their pictures people busy at some everyday occupation. Farmers at work in their fields, city people riding on a bus, factory workers in the mills, shoppers on bargain day are subjects which artists have chosen to paint. People on a holiday is another theme which artists sometimes paint. The next picture shows how an artist who lived about four hundred years ago used this theme.

"The Wedding Dance," by Brughel

In a painting you may see in a library collection, peasants of four hundred years ago are celebrating a wedding. Pieter Breughel (Pē-ā'ter Brü'gel), the artist, was a peasant, and he liked to paint people as he saw them on such occasions as this. He is called Pieter Breughel, the Elder, because his son Pieter was also an artist, as well as his younger son, Jan. Pieter, the Elder, is considered the greatest artist of the three. Notice how he painted the human figure. The forms are solidly constructed. We can almost imagine them as little wooden figures. Breughel was clever at using many figures in one picture. Here he has dozens of them but there is no effect of confusion or lack of unity. Notice also that the scene is painted as though viewed from a height. This is a scheme often used by modern painters.

The color in "The Wedding Dance" is as gay and jolly as the occasion which is the subject of the picture. A strong "dark and light" pattern is made lively with color. Strong reds and whites dominate the color scheme, fine yellows and tans are secondary in emphasis, and rich blues are third in order of importance. Dull greens and browns are woven through the composition with unifying and harmonious effect. The whole combination is vigorous, delightful. Note how the plan fits in with ideas learned in your study of color contrasts and harmonies.

Dramatic and Exciting Subjects—Three Pictures

Sometimes artists choose subjects that are dramatic and exciting. Moments of danger and tragedy expressed in paint can be as exciting as on the stage or screen. In our last three pictures we shall see how three American artists have used a fog at sea, a tornado, and a prize fight as subjects for exciting and dramatic pictures.

"The Fog Warning," by Winslow Homer

This painting in Figure 100 gives us another exciting moment. A fisherman in his boat sees the fog approaching. He is far from the schooner, which he must reach for safety. We can just see it in the distance and the fog that is rolling up behind it. If the schooner is hidden by the fog, the fisherman will have no way to find it except by listening for the foghorn. It is a dangerous situation. The fisherman's little dory is tossed about like a cork by the giant waves. We wonder that the fisherman can take it safely across the mountainous waves even without the extra danger of the perilous fog.

In "The Fog Warning" Homer has given us a dramatic moment from a real situation. He is called a realist because he tried

FIGURE 100. "The Fog Warning," by Winslow Homer.

COURTESY, MUSEUM OF FINE ARTS, BOSTON

to show us nature exactly as it is. He never changed anything in order to get a more dramatic picture. When he was asked if he ever took the liberty of modifying any form or color in nature, he replied, "Never! Never! When I have selected the thing carefully I paint it exactly as it appears."

You see there are different ways of securing dramatic effects in pictures. El Greco got his by changing, distorting, and twisting forms and by putting them into imaginary situations. Homer achieved his by first finding a truly dramatic effect in nature and then painting it exactly as it appeared. It is easy to see why Homer's kind of painting is called realism.

When he was middle-aged, Homer retired to a wild headland off the Maine coast. There he built a cottage in which he lived during the summer months. During the winter he lived and painted in Florida. He studied the sea tirelessly. He waited for months and months to study certain wave formations. He built a portable cabin at his home on the Maine coast which could be moved about. Thus he could study the storms at sea and paint what he saw on the spot. He especially liked to paint man's struggle against the overwhelming power of the sea.

"The Fog Warning" was originally called "Halibut Fishing." Which name suits the picture better? Why?

"Tornado Over Kansas," by Curry

From storms on the Atlantic coast we go to a storm on the western prairies. "Tornado Over Kansas," by John Steuart Curry, Figure 101, tells its own story. A great, swirling funnel rushes over the prairie toward the farm home. The big farmer holding his little girl by the hand, looks back, urging the boys to hurry. The boys are running, one carrying a clawing black cat, the other two little pigs. The mother. holding the baby and wide-eyed with apprehension, is just entering the cyclone cellar. It is all swift, dramatic movement. It catches the fearful moment before the tornado strikes.

Curry grew up on a Kansas farm, and he painted this picture from his memories of tornados in his boyhood. His favorite subjects for painting are farm animals, storms, and rural scenes from the Middle West, especially Kansas.

"Dempsey and Firpo," by George Bellows

Another American artist, George Bellows, has given us another kind of dramatic picture. His painting called "Dempsey and Firpo," Figure 102, shows us a powerfully dramatic moment in

FIGURE 101. *"The Tornado," by John Steuart Curry.*

COURTESY, HACKLEY ART GALLERY

a famous prize fight. Jack Dempsey, as you probably know, held the championship for heavyweights. He was challenged by Louis Angel Firpo, a South American of tremendous strength, sometimes called the Wild Bull of the Pampas. Dempsey won the fight but during the battle Firpo managed to knock Dempsey right through the ropes into the laps of some spectators. Such a thing had never happened before and this is the moment that Bellows chose to portray. It is a picture of furious action and terrific excitement.

Bellows was a good athlete himself. In fact he almost became a professional baseball player instead of an artist. He painted several exciting pictures of prizefights, polo games, and other sports. But he could also paint quiet pictures. Sometime you

FIGURE 102. "Dempsey and Firpo," by George Bellows.

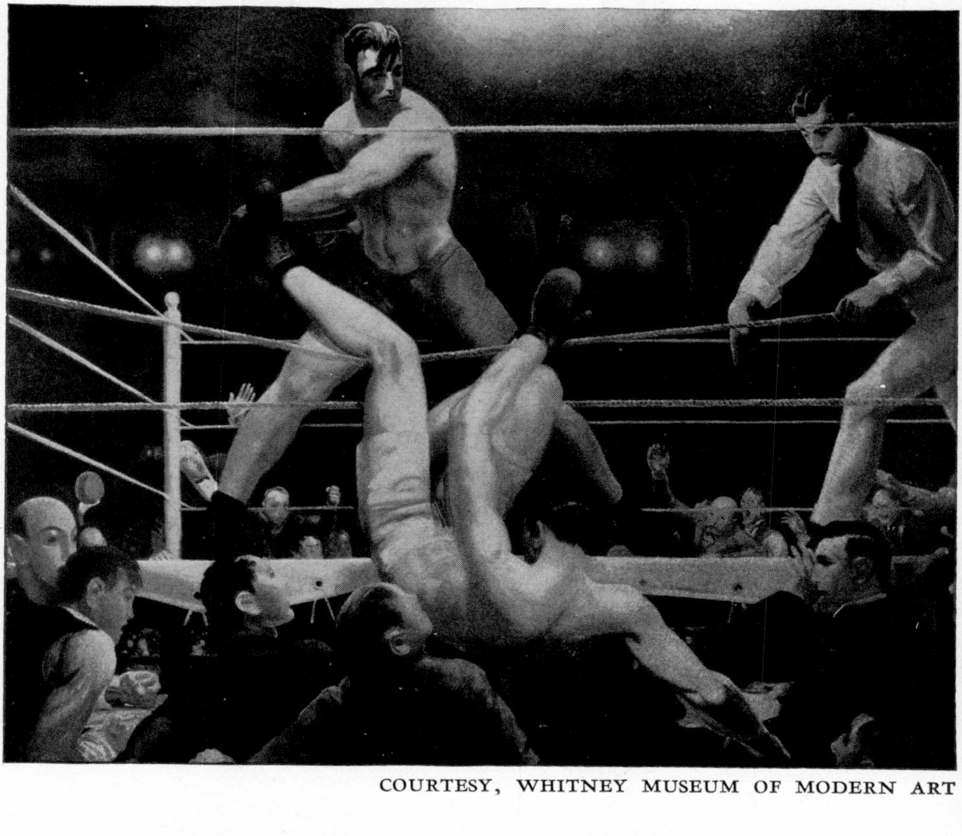

COURTESY, WHITNEY MUSEUM OF MODERN ART

will become acquainted with his very fine portraits of his mother and his children.

From your study of "Dempsey and Firpo" would you say that Bellows' work is realistic, romantic, or imaginative? Why?

A Survey of Your Private Picture Gallery

You have now added fifteen paintings to the picture gallery in your head. You probably never will own any of these canvases but you need never forget them. Because you have become acquainted with them you have had an art experience that is interesting and enjoyable. Moreover, no one can take away from you your enjoyment of these pictures. It is something you cannot lose! You can return to them again and again with the same pleasure, and the memory of them goes with you.

Now look over your fifteen pictures and decide which one you like best. Of course, you may like them all but still like one a little better than the others. It is always a good plan to pick out your favorite picture in an art gallery. *But* this should not mean that you cannot also enjoy other kinds of pictures.

Take a class vote on the following:

1. Which of the fifteen pictures in this chapter do you like best?
2. What subject for paintings do you prefer, landscape, portrait, human figure, cities and buildings, or dramatic pictures?
3. If you were a painter living in your present community, what would you choose to paint?

EXPERIENCES IN APPRECIATION

1. Learn to know other landscapes by one of the three landscape artists mentioned in this chapter. The references at the end of this book and your teacher will help you to look up reference materials. Be prepared to report to the class on the artist you select.

2. Why can the Barbizon school be called an outdoors movement in painting?

3. Become acquainted with the work of any landscape painter living in your own community. If possible, ask the painter to paint a picture before your class and to tell you how he works.

4. Select a place and time in your part of the country which you think would be a good subject for a landscape painter. Which of the landscape painters studied do you think could do the best job of painting the subject? Would it be a romantic landscape like Corot's, one symbolizing a meaning like Kent's, or a decorative one like Grant Wood's? What features of the landscape would you expect your artist to emphasize?

5. Select a spot in your town which you think would be a good subject for Burchfield to paint; one for Jonas Lie to paint; one for Warner to paint. What quality would you expect to see made important in each case?

6. Would you rather have John W. Alexander or Zuloaga paint your portrait? Why?

7. Learn to know other pictures by Rembrandt, especially "The Night Watch," his portraits of Saskia, and his portraits of old men and women.

8. Create in words an imaginary picture of some dramatic event in modern times which you would like to see painted by Bellows.

9. Learn to know other paintings by Winslow Homer, particularly his water colors of the Southern Atlantic coast.

10. Try and look at the world with the eyes of an artist. Artists see in many different ways. Select the artist who paints as you would like to paint. Then try to see your own community through his eyes. Report any interesting experience you have because of this attempt to see the world as an artist.

11. Visit a picture exhibition if there is one in your town.

CREATIVE ACTIVITIES

1. Plan to paint a series of pictures called "People and Places That I Know." These pictures might include portraits of your family and friends, street scenes and neighborhood scenes, landscapes of places that you like, interior views of your own home, especially in your own room, and scenes in your school and church.

Each picture should be thought out carefully before you begin to paint. Do not attempt to do too many. It is better to paint two good pictures than ten poor ones.

Remember to have a center of interest in each picture and to fill the space in an interesting way.

2. Draw a dramatic picture. First, be sure to select a truly exciting event; second, decide what view will be most effective; third, choose colors and contrasts of light and dark that are exciting.

3. Plan a mural which you think would be suitable for a room in your school. Choose a subject which has special meaning in your community. Use 9 x 12 paper for your mural and attach the pieces so as to make a strip as long as you wish it to be.

10

BEAUTIFUL BUILDINGS, OLD AND NEW

W*E HAVE FOUND* beauty in many forms, in trees and posters, in machines and animals, in pictures and statues. Yet there is still another important form in which we may find beauty. It is in buildings. Architecture or the art of building is considered one of the major arts and it is here that we have a chance to enjoy beauty in one of its finest forms. Buildings, old or new, large or small, public or private, provide many opportunities for study and pleasure.

Perhaps when you are older, some of you will become architects. In that case you will read many books and study many years to learn how to plan buildings. Then possibly you will design some of the world's great architecture.

But whether you become an architect or not, you should learn to enjoy beautiful buildings. In this chapter we shall get merely a glimpse of the world's splendid architecture. Since we live in America we should be acquainted with our own famous buildings. This chapter will introduce to you American buildings and famous buildings in other countries which are really the ancestors of our own American buildings.

A Greek Temple—The Parthenon

The picture in Figure 103 shows all that is now left of an old

FIGURE 103. The Greek Parthenon as it appears today

Greek Temple built in Athens and finished in the year 438 B. C. Historians have called this building the most famous in the world, and architects have called it the most perfect building ever built. Time has not dealt kindly with this beautiful old building. As you can see, it is now a ruin with only the outer columns still standing. The picture in Figure 104 will give you a better idea of how the Parthenon looked when it was first constructed. This building is a copy of the old Parthenon and was erected in Centennial Park, Nashville, Tennessee. It is used as an art gallery. Naturally it is one of the sights of Nashville, and it is worth seeing both for its beauty and for the historical interest in the original Greek building.

First, we shall learn the story of what happened to the Parthenon from the time it was finished until the present, and then we shall discuss its beauty. It was finished in 438 B. C., which means that it is now almost 2,400 years old. The temple was intended for the worship of Athena, the favorite and special goddess of the people of Athens. Although the Greek temple was a place of

187

PHOTOGRAPH BY EWING GALLOWAY, NEW YORK

FIGURE 104. The Parthenon in Nashville, Tenn., which was copied after the old Greek Parthenon.

worship, just as our churches today are places of worship, the temple was not planned or used at all like our churches. We go to Sunday School and to church services on Sunday, and we may go to parties or meetings any day of the week. In the church we find chairs, organs, and many other furnishings. There was nothing like this in a Greek temple. The people were not expected to attend regular services. There were no chairs or seats for people inside the temple, not even a meeting hall. Mostly people stood outside the temple and looked in at the open doorway. On special occasions they were permitted inside, especially if they brought gifts to the goddess.

There were only two rooms in the Parthenon and not even a doorway between. The big room at the eastern end was the sacred room. They said this room was the earthly home of the goddess. This made it a sacred place, and ordinary human beings would not go into a sacred place without a special reason. To do so might anger the goddess! It would be sacrilege. Instead people would stand at the open doorway and look in at the great, golden statue of Athena. It was a giant statue covered with gold and ivory. No wonder people were impressed when they looked into the beautiful room with its marble floor, walls, and columns, and most of all its great, gold statue.

The room at the other end of the Parthenon was smaller and generally kept locked because it was here that were kept the valuable presents which the people brought as offerings to Athena. Such gifts as gold, jewels, embroideries, and perfumes could be kept and were stored in the treasury room at the western end. Every four years there was a great celebration called the Pantheanaic festival when people from all parts of Greece brought offerings to Athena. After two days of games and feasting in the city, the people formed into a great procession and climbed the long, winding road to the top of the hill, called the Acropolis, where the Parthenon stands. The story of this procession is told in the sculptured frieze around the top of the wall inside the colonnade.

Students in the ancient history class can make a report about the Parthenon in the days of ancient Athens.

The Parthenon was used as a temple for the worship of Athena until about the fifth century A. D. This was a period of approximately 800 years. By the fifth century most of the people in Athens had been converted to the Christian religion. They no longer wanted a temple with a golden idol in their city. The Parthenon was changed into a Christian church. The golden statue of Athena was taken to Constantinople for safe keeping. No one knows now what finally happened to it. Perhaps it was broken up for the valuable materials in it, or perhaps it was destroyed in the great fire of Constantinople. The main entrance to the Parthenon was changed to the western end, seats and a pulpit were installed, and a doorway was cut between the two rooms. Then for about 1,000 years the Parthenon was used as a church. Then came the time when the Turks from the east invaded Athens and gained possession of the city. Theirs was a different religion and they did not wish to have a Christian church, so they changed the Parthenon into their kind of church, called a mosque. Now a mosque must have a cupola on the eastern end, so the Turks built one onto the eastern end of the temple.

Remember that all this time the Parthenon remained strong and stood firmly on its hill. Finally after another two centuries, in 1687, the Venetians from the west came to drive the Turks back home. The Turks were hard pressed and retreated to the top of the Acropolis to make a last stand. They looked about for a safe, dry place to keep their gunpowder and ammunition. Thinking that the enemy would not fire upon a building so old and famous, especially one that had been used for a church, the Turks decided to store their gunpowder in the Parthenon. Perhaps it would have been all right but a deserter from the Turkish army got away and went to the Venetian general and told him where the gunpowder was stored. The general said he hated to do it but he ordered his cannons turned upon the Parthenon. Four cannon shots hit the building in rapid succession. There was a tremendous explosion. The Parthenon stood in ruins.

Such a history would make any building famous, but the Parthenon is also famous for its beauty. Perhaps this is hard for you to see when you are looking at the ruins in Figure 103. However, you will be able to see its loveliness in the reproduction of the original building pictured in Figure 104. First, notice the fine proportions. To make the building a bit higher or longer or wider would spoil the effect. It seems exactly right. Next, notice the splendid columns that form a colonnade around the building. They are lovely and perfect. We have no feeling that they are merely posts stuck up to support the roof. They are beautiful in form and proportion. You will observe that each column is wider at the base than at the top, and that the sides curve *very slightly*. This makes them graceful and yet strong. It makes them seem to grow from the step upon which they rest. If they were a bit heavier they would seem clumsy and if they were a bit thinner they would seem weak. If the sides were more curved the effect would be bulky, and if they had been perfectly straight the effect would have been stiff. The grooves or fluting on the columns adds to the lovely, graceful effect.

The triangular space under the roof at each end of the temple is called a pediment. On the Parthenon each pediment is filled with splendid sculpture. The group of statues in each pediment tells a story about the gods which the ancient Greeks believed to be true. Perhaps you can learn these stories in your history or literature class. There is more sculptured decoration in the rectangular panels called metopes, which make a border around the top of the building. You will notice that these metopes are separated by plain panels with vertical grooves. These panels are called triglyphs.

A problem in proportions: The metopes and triglyphs are not the same width. Why not? How would it have spoiled the effect to make them all the same size?

The top part of a column is called a capital. On these columns the capital consists of a circular, bell-shaped collar called the echinus and a square block called the abacus. On these capitals rests the upper structure.

What artistic purpose do these capitals serve besides adding a little decoration? For help in answering look at the discussion of airplane design on page 26.

There is much more to be learned about the Parthenon, but we must save time to become acquainted with other fine buildings.

Greek Columns—Doric, Ionic, Corinthian

The ancient Greeks invented three different designs in columns which they used on their temples and other buildings. Since these three styles of columns have been copied by other peoples ever since the Greeks invented them, it is worth while for us to learn them. You will undoubtedly find examples of one or more of them in your own community, perhaps on your own front porch.

The style used on the Parthenon is called Doric. It is the plainest and simplest of the three styles and it has the plainest name. Remember that the bottom rests directly on the step with no extra base, and the capital consists only of the round echinus and the square abacus. The first diagram in Figure 105 shows the design of the Doric column.

The second style of column designed by the Greeks is the Ionic. See the second diagram in Figure 105. You will notice at once that the column is more slender. It is not so strong looking but it is more graceful. It has a base made up of circular blocks. The capital is the most distinguishing feature. The two spirals are called volutes. One story says that the architect got his idea for this capital from the way a ram's horns curl around. Another story says he got his idea from the way the Greek women did their hair in two coils at the neck. Possibly neither story is true but they are interesting to know. Sometimes the Ionic column is called the woman's column, perhaps because of the story about the women's hairdress and perhaps because the columns are more slender and graceful than the Doric.

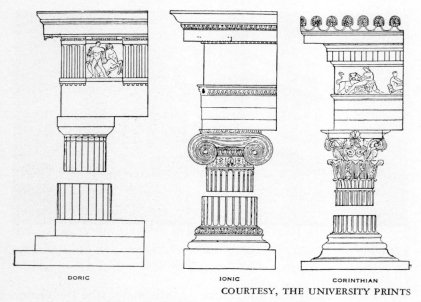

DORIC   IONIC   CORINTHIAN

COURTESY, THE UNIVERSITY PRINTS

FIGURE 105. The three styles in Greek columns.

The third style of Greek column is the Corinthian. It is shown in the third diagram in Figure 105. This is much the fanciest of the three styles. It also has the fanciest name. Possibly that will help you to keep it straight in your memory. This style also has volutes but they are smaller than in the Ionic style. Below the little volutes are acanthus leaves curling outward around the neck of the column. A story says that the architect got his idea from something he saw in a cemetery. A basket of toys had been set upon a child's grave. It happened to be placed upon an acanthus plant, which grew around the basket and suggested the design.

The Greeks did not like fancy things very well, so they did not often use Corinthian columns on their temples, but the Romans, who copied from the Greeks, did like fancy designs, so they used the Corinthian style a great deal. Probably you have learned from

PHOTOGRAPH BY C. O. BUCKINGHAM CO., INC.

FIGURE 106. The Lincoln Memorial in Washington, D. C., is patterned after the Parthenon.

your history study that the Romans finally conquered the Greeks and copied from them their sculpture and architecture. So we have Roman Doric, Ionic, and Corinthian styles. These are not exactly like the Greek styles but they are similar.

> List the buildings in your community where Doric, Ionic, and Corinthian columns are used.

A Greek Temple in America—The Lincoln Memorial

At one end of the reflecting pool in Potomac Park, Washington, D. C., stands a splendid memorial to Abraham Lincoln. See Figure 106. It is patterned after a Greek temple, in the Doric style. It is surrounded by a colonnade of thirty-six beautiful columns, one column for each of the thirty-six states in the union when Lincoln was president. Inside is the great statue of Lincoln by Daniel Chester French with which we became acquainted in our study of famous sculpture, Figure 78. The impressive statue in its beautiful setting makes a shrine which many thousands of Amer-

icans visit every year. If you have been there, you will know
that people who enter the memorial are so impressed with its
beauty and meaning that they stand before it in silence.

Why is the Doric style particularly well suited for a memorial to Abraham
Lincoln?

Are there any buildings in your town that you think are patterned after a
Greek temple?

A Famous Roman Building—The Pantheon

It is said that the Greeks were the greater architects and that
the Romans were the greater builders. The Romans copied de-

FIGURE 107. *The Pantheon, in Rome, Italy.*

PHOTOGRAPH BY EWING GALLOWAY, NEW YORK

signs from Greek architecture but they also used types of construction which the Greeks did not use. The round arch, the dome, and the vault were used frequently in Roman architecture. In your history class probably you have learned about the aqueducts which brought mountain spring water to Rome. These were supported by a series of round, stone arches. You may also know the great Roman amphitheater called the Colosseum. It is an elliptical building with three tiers of arched openings all around.

The Pantheon, Figure 107, in Rome is one of the world's truly impressive buildings. It was originally built as a temple to all the gods but was later transformed into a Christian church. As you can see it is constructed with a great dome. To support this dome the walls were made twenty feet thick. There are no windows, and light is admitted only through a circular opening in the center of the dome. People who visit the building are thrilled with its great size and spaciousness. They marvel at the Romans who nearly 2,000 years ago could build such a structure.

> Do you know any bridges in America that suggest the aqueduct? Or any stadium that suggests the Colosseum? Or any buildings with domes?

Roman Buildings in America

Undoubtedly you have learned about Thomas Jefferson as a great statesman and as the third president of the United States. Did you also learn that he was a fine architect? He designed several buildings which are still famous for their beauty. One of them is his own home in Virginia. He called it Monticello, meaning "little mountain," because it was built on the top of a big hill which he leveled off for the building. Jefferson spent several years in France and there came to admire Greek and Roman architecture. When he returned to this country he used these styles in the buildings he designed. Monticello, shown in Figure 108, has

*FIGURE 108. Monticello, the home of Thomas Jefferson, is Roman-like
in character.*

a Roman dome over the center part of the house. Perhaps it does
not seem truly Roman in type because he was forced to use brick
instead of the white marble which the Romans used. However,
it is very Roman-like in its style.

Not far away from Monticello is the city of Charlottesville.
Here stand the buildings of the University of Virginia. The university was Jefferson's idea because he believed in education for
everyone. He designed the buildings and in them even more than
in Monticello you can trace the influence of Roman architecture.

Not all Roman buildings carried domes. Many of them were
built very much like Greek temples, as you will know if you are
familiar with pictures of the Roman forums and temples.

Is there any building in your town which you think was patterned
after Roman architecture? Why?

Classical Architecture in America

In reading about American architecture you will sometimes find
a reference to the classic style or to the classical influence. You

PHOTOGRAPH BY EWING GALLOWAY, NEW YORK

FIGURE 109. The Capitol building in Washington, D. C.

are already acquainted with this style because classical is merely another name for Greek and Roman styles. The Lincoln Memorial and Monticello are classic style.

A very famous building in classic style is the Capitol in Washington, D. C. In Figure 109 you can see the beautiful dome which dominates the great masses of the building below. Every American knows this building and likes it, not only because it is beautiful but because it stands for the American way of government. It is a symbol of our fine, great country. Thousands of people visit it every year, so perhaps you have seen it. No one can help but be impressed by the huge size, the marble steps, the porticos, and most of all the dome which towers above the building.

The classic style has been used for many government buildings both in Washington and in state capitals. Someone has said that we can hardly govern without a dome! Of course, this is only a joke, for there are many fine government buildings without domes.

How many government buildings in your state are built in the classic style? Collect pictures of them.

Ask the coöperation of your history teacher in learning the story of the national capitol, how it was built, who designed it, and other interesting features.

The National Gallery of Art in Washington is a new building in the old classic style. It was opened to the public in March, 1941, but it is designed in a style that was originated more than 2,000 years ago. In Figure 110 you can see the entrance, which is similar in appearance to the front of the Pantheon (see Figure 107). The National Gallery also has a great rotunda which again is somewhat similar to that of the Pantheon. This building houses a great collection of old masterpieces of sculpture and painting. It seems suitable that a historic style of architecture was selected for a building which contains an important collection of historic art.

What style of architecture was used for the art galleries and museums in your own community, or which you have visited?

Styles in Buildings Change, but Not Often

Styles in architecture change just as style in ladies' hats change, but not nearly so often. We expect new styles in millinery every year but not in buildings. In the past an architectural style has lasted for several hundred years. There may be minor variations but the general style remains the same. The Greek style lasted at least 500 years. The Roman style which followed it (and partly copied from it) also lasted for many hundreds of years. After the

FIGURE 110. The National Gallery of Art in Washington, D. C., is patterned after the Roman Pantheon.

fall of the Roman Empire in 476 A. D. there was not much build-ing in Europe for 800 years. Most people were poor and lived unhappy, miserable lives. This period in history is sometimes called the Dark Ages. Under such conditions we could not expect much fine building. Such great buildings as were erected were mostly churches and church buildings.

FIGURE 111. The cloistered courtyard from the old monastery at Saint Michel-de-Cuxa in France, which has been moved and reconstructed in New York City.

The Romanesque Style

These churches were copied more or less from the Roman style and so they are called Romanesque (Roman-esk'), meaning Roman-like. In a style copied from the Roman, we naturally will find round arches, domes, columns, and porticos. A few new features were also added. Some of these are towers, courtyards, and cloisters. The picture in Figure 111 shows the famous Cuxa Cloister. A passageway between a wall and a row of arches (arcade) is known as a cloister. The word cloister is also used as a name for a courtyard surrounded by cloistered walls. Cloister may also refer to the whole monastery or nunnery. The Cuxa Cloister shown in Figure 111 is the courtyard from the old monastery at Saint Michel-de-Cuxa in southwestern France. This is a restoration which is located in the museum in New York City known as "The

Cloisters." Parts of the ruined Cuxa Cloister in France were brought to New York, and other parts were made in the same style so that the cloister could be reconstructed as accurately as possible. The result is very beautiful. If you sometime make a trip to New York City, visit "The Cloisters" and see the Cuxa Cloister. It is easy to imagine the monks walking and talking with each other in passageways and the garden court.

Notice that the columns and capitals differ from any of the Greek or Roman styles. No two of them are exactly alike. Lions, apes, birds, grapes, human figures, and many other conventionalized forms are used in the design of these interesting capitals.

The Romanesque style has been used in America although not so much as the classic. Some of the famous Romanesque buildings in this country are the statehouse at Albany, the courthouse at Pittsburgh, and Trinity Church in Boston. A number of churches in America are Romanesque in style. Perhaps there are some in your own town.

The Gothic Style—Then and Now

After about 800 years of Romanesque, a new style in architecture appeared. This was in the thirteenth century. You can see what this new style is like in Figure 112, which shows you a view of the Notre Dame Cathedral in Paris. At first, people did not like this new style in buildings. They liked the old style and were satisfied with it. So they made fun of the new architecture and said it looked as though the Goths had done it. Now, the Goths were barbarians who roamed the plains of Europe and were not smart enough to build a great cathedral which would stand strong and beautiful. When people said the new style was Gothic they meant it was barbaric. After awhile people changed their minds and began to like this strange new style in buildings. But the

FIGURE 112. The Notre Dame Cathedral in Paris, France.

name was never changed and so we call it Gothic to this very day.

Let us pick out the special characteristics of the Gothic style. You can see these features in the pictures of the Paris cathedral.

1. Pointed arches. This is quite different from the round arches of the Romanesque style.

2. Spires and turrets. These show best in the rear view of the Paris cathedral. The towers on the façade (face) were meant to be finished with spires but so many years passed before the cathedral was completed that the spires have never been added.

3. Flying buttresses. These graceful arched supports brace the main wall and keep it from buckling outward from the weight of the roof. Remember, there was no steel construction to strengthen big buildings when these cathedrals were built.

4. Traceried windows. The great windows are cut into lovely and intricate patterns with stone framework. This strengthens the window frames and makes them more beautiful. The round windows are called rose windows.

203

5. Stained-glass windows. The great windows of the Gothic cathedrals were stained glass. Generally they told stories from the Bible, such as the Wise Men following the star to Bethlehem.

6. Gargoyles and grotesques. Many Gothic cathedrals are decorated with queer little, stone figures such as those shown in Figure 113. The figures in the second picture are really decorative rain spouts, and serve to carry away the rainwater from the roof. The little figures are elongated so that the water will not fall too near the wall. You can see the little troughs and the open mouths through which the water runs. Because of the gurgling noise made by the water, these figures have been called "gurgles" or gargoyles (pronounced gär'goils). The grotesque figure in the first picture of Figure 113 is not a rain spout, but may have been considered useful by the people who built the cathedral. It is said that the people of the Middle Ages believed that these grotesques would frighten away the evil spirits. The gargoyles and the grotesque in Figure 113 are from Notre Dame in Paris, which is famous for these little stone figures.

7. The vaulted roof. The interior of a Gothic cathedral shows

FIGURE 113. A grotesque figure (left) and two gargoyles (right) from Notre Dame Cathedral in Paris.

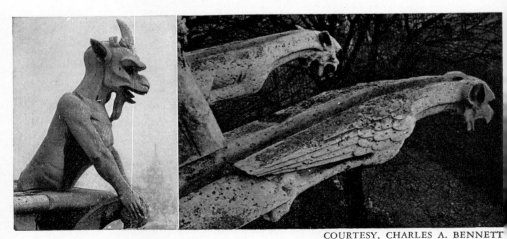

COURTESY, CHARLES A. BENNETT

the framework of pointed arches which support the roof and towers.

Remember that the old Gothic cathedrals were built entirely from stone. There are thousands of Gothic buildings in America today but most of them were built with a steel framework. Steel structure makes possible taller and heavier towers than with only stone construction. One of the famous, modern Gothic buildings in America is the University of Pittsburgh, known as the Cathedral of Learning, Figure 114. Note how the vertical lines are emphasized in the design of this building. It is really a modern skyscraper.

Near to the mighty Cathedral of Learning is a tiny, Gothic building called the Heinz Chapel, Figure 115. This little chapel is as lovely as anything one could imagine. It is patterned after the famous church in Paris called San Chapelle. It has been said that Gothic spires reach to Heaven. Does not this beautiful, dainty spire reach toward Heaven? See how the lovely little turrets echo the skyward thrust.

There are thousands of Gothic buildings in America. Most of them are churches. Perhaps it is the upward movement in the Gothic design which makes it seem especially well suited to church architecture.

How many Gothic buildings do you know in your own community? Make a class list.

What other architectural style can you see in Figure 115?

The Revival of an Old Style—The Renaissance

For about 200 years, the Gothic style was used for practically all important buildings. Then in the fifteenth century another style became popular. But it was not an entirely new style—it was really a revival of the old classic style. It imitated Greek and

FIGURE 114.   The University of Pittsburgh, often called
"The Cathedral of Learning."

Roman architecture. This new style was called Renaissance, which
means rebirth. In other words, the Renaissance style was a rebirth of the Greek and Roman styles. However, it had a new way
of using the old classic style and is really a distinct style.

The Riccardi Palace in Florence, Italy, is a Renaissance building
of the fifteenth century. See Figure 116. Some people think it

FIGURE 115. The Heinz Chapel, University of Pittsburgh; a modern
building in the Gothic style.

FIGURE 116. The Riccardi Palace, built in Florence, Italy during the Renaissance.

looks more like a prison than a palace. Remember that in the days when this palace was built, rich men needed strong houses in which to keep their valuable possessions. It was their protection against robbers, and against mobs belonging to another political party.

One of the best-known Renaissance buildings in America is the Boston Public Library. See Figure 117. In its design you can see some of the same features used in the Riccardi Palace. Characteristics of Renaissance architecture are round arches, round-headed windows, domes, colossal-size columns reaching several stories, heavy projecting cornices, balustrades (heavy stone railings), symmetrical plan, and ornamentation of scrolls, garlands, shields, and cupids. Not every Renaissance building shows all these characteristics. For example, neither the Riccardi Palace nor the Boston Public Library has a dome. St. Peter's in Rome is a very famous Renaissance building with a dome. See Figure 118. It is also much more fancy and elaborate in design than the Riccardi Palace.

What Renaissance buildings can you find in your own community?

The Georgian Style—Really Renaissance

Georgian is a name which was given to Renaissance architecture in England. It is called Georgian because this style of archi-

FIGURE 117. The Boston Public Library is patterned after the Renaissance style.

PHOTOGRAPH BY EWING GALLOWAY, NEW YORK

*FIGURE 118. St. Peter's Cathedral in Rome, Italy, was built
during the Renaissance.*

tecture was popular during a period when three English kings,
George I, George II, and George III, were rulers, one after another. It was also during this period that the American colonies
were growing and developing. Plans and drawings of English
Georgian architecture were brought to America. The natural
result was Georgian buildings in the American Colonies. You
see how, by a round about way, Renaissance architecture, which
started in Italy, reached America. It is called Georgian Colonial,
or more often just Colonial.

Probably you are already familiar with the most famous Georgian Colonial building in America. It is Independence Hall in
Philadelphia. Figure 119. Here the Declaration of Independence

was signed, and here you see the Liberty Bell which rang so hard
that it cracked. Of course, you have learned its story in your history class. This Renaissance style does not look much like the
Italian Renaissance buildings, the Riccardi Palace, or St. Peter's.
Georgian Colonial was made to suit the needs of the place where

FIGURE 119. Independence Hall in Philadelphia.

PHOTOGRAPH BY EWING GALLOWAY, NEW YORK

it was built. It could not be great and pretentious like St. Peter's and it need not be so prisonlike as the Riccardi Palace. Yet we can see the same features used in another way. It is symmetrical in form. The windows are regularly spaced. Balustrades decorate the top of the building. The tower has a dome-like top. Round arches are used in the tower openings.

You are probably acquainted with other Georgian Colonial buildings through your history study. Mount Vernon, home of George Washington, is a famous Colonial building which is visited by many thousands of people every year. If you have the opportunity to see it, remember to look at it carefully because it is a beautiful building as well as a famous one.

Buildings which were erected after the Revolutionary War cannot properly be called Georgian, although they are not much different in style. Monticello and the University of Virginia buildings, which we studied earlier, were done mostly after the Revolution, but you will remember that Jefferson's inspiration was Greek and Roman architecture. Therefore, it is not strange that his buildings are similar in style to the English Georgian.

Is there any Georgian Colonial architecture in your locality? Is it historic or a modern copy?

Spanish-Mission Architecture in America

Most Colonial architecture is found in the eastern part of the United States. This is natural because that is where the colonies were settled. Another type of architecture is common in the southwestern part of the United States, and it is interesting to know why it is there. Mexico and part of the southwestern states were first settled by the Spanish. Later, about the time the Revolutionary War was being fought in the East, the Franciscan monks were building missions in California. These missions were something like the monasteries of the Middle Ages, with the church and other buildings grouped about a cloistered court. The Franciscans built a chain of these missions along the seacoast, a day's journey apart. The old mission at Santa Barbara is shown in Figure 120 A. These missions were built from adobe, or sun-dried brick. Generally, the mission had one or two towers with round, arched openings. In the Santa Barbara Mission the towers are crowned with domes. Notice especially the interesting spacing of these towers. The bottom space is the greatest, the next is shorter, and the top space still shorter. It makes a very pleasing variety of proportions.

In Figure 120 B a modern building in Spanish style is pictured. It is the Santa Barbara County Courthouse. Certainly it is one of the most interesting public buildings in America. The people chose to use a style of architecture that is important historically in their community. At the same time the building is beautiful and well suited to serve the need for a county courthouse in this part of the country.

There are many modern buildings in California patterned after the Spanish-Mission style. It is not only beautiful but well suited to the climate. Small windows shut out the glaring sunlight, and the patios and courtyards make pleasant, outdoor, living places. There are also many Spanish style buildings in Texas and Florida. Perhaps you will remember from your history work that the Spanish settled in Florida in the early days of this country.

Ask your social studies teacher to help you learn the story of Fort Marion at St. Augustine, Florida.

Modern Styles of Architecture

New styles in architecture do not happen very often. We have skipped rapidly over the centuries since the days of the ancient

PHOTOGRAPH BY J. WALTER COLLINGE

A

PHOTOGRAPH BY J. WALTER COLLINGE

B

FIGURE 120. *A. The old Spanish Mission at Santa Barbara, California. B. The modern courthouse, Santa Barbara, California, is designed in the historic Spanish style.*

214

Greeks and found only six different architectural styles used in western Europe and in America. These are Greek, Roman, Romanesque, Gothic, Renaissance, and Spanish Mission. Of course, there are variations of these styles which we have not had time to study. Later you probably will learn about other styles used in eastern Europe, Asia, and northern Africa. To finish our present discussion of architectural styles we shall learn about the one that has happened in our own time. It is still very new in the history of world architecture, so it has no name except *modern*. We may well wonder what it will be called 2,000 years from now. Perhaps it will be called "Twentieth Century."

The first skyscraper was built in Chicago in 1890. That is not very long ago when we are thinking about styles in architecture. This first skyscraper was not very tall, only ten stories, but it was the beginning of a new style. However, the first skyscrapers were made to resemble some historic style. Greek columns, domes, Gothic trimmings were added to the structures. This was not really good style because skyscrapers are not adapted to the same materials or type of construction as the historic styles. Skyscrapers depend on steel construction. Architects say that the exterior of a building should not conceal the way it is made, but show its structure. Therefore, the exterior of a skyscraper should suggest the steel structure underneath. Historic styles could not do this.

Eventually a style of architecture was developed that does suggest the steel structure. Look at the skyscraper shown in Figure 121. It is the group of buildings at Rockefeller Center, New York City. It is easy to feel that underneath the mass of stone and concrete are great steel beams which support the structure. There are no decorations or cornices to stop the eye as it travels up and down the skyscraper. Only the rows of windows form a pattern of dark against light. The upper parts of the buildings in

Rockefeller Center are set back from the street. This is because of a zoning law which does not allow the skyscrapers to rise straight up from the sidewalk above a certain height. Yet these setbacks undoubtedly add to the pleasing effect.

When the exterior design of a building shows how it is constructed, the style is sometimes called functional. Perhaps in the future our steel-and-concrete skyscrapers will be called Functional. Or perhaps they will be called American. Such tall buildings would never have been as practicable had it not been for steel, concrete, and electricity. Steel and concrete are necessary for strength in these tall buildings. Electricity is used, most of all, for lighting and in order to operate elevators.

The building in Figure 122 is the helio-laboratory for the Johnson Wax Company in Racine, Wisconsin. It was designed by the most famous of contemporary architects, Frank Lloyd Wright. The design is based on a new type of construction which allows a maximum amount of sun and air to reach every room on every floor. The word helio is derived from the name of the Greek sun god, Helios, so helio-laboratory means a sun-laboratory. A giant stack or core of reinforced concrete goes up through the center of the building, and the floors are cantilevers from this central core, spreading out like the branches of a tree. This core can be seen in the picture underneath the bottom floor.

Now from skyscrapers and towers we shall go to art galleries in the modern style. The building shown in Figure 123 is the Museum of Modern Art in New York City. It is a five-story building made of steel, glass, and reinforced concrete. Notice the plain walls and ribbonlike windows. The design is characterized by severe, horizontal lines. The style is especially distinctive here because the building is sandwiched in between two buildings of older style. The whole building is functional in design.

FIGURE 121. *Rockefeller Center in New York City. The tallest structure is the RCA building.*

217

FIGURE 122. The Helio-Laboratory of the Johnson Wax
Company at Racine, Wisconsin. It is dramatic in
effect, especially at night.

218

FIGURE 123. *The Museum of Modern Art, New York City.*

219

*This interesting modern design was created for St. Scholastica's
Church in Aspinwall, Pennsylvania.*

220

The beautiful modern style church on page 224A is St. Scholastica's in Aspinwall, Pennsylvania. You will observe that the design is made up of rectangular shapes and forms which merge in wonderfully harmonious effect.   In place of the traditional stained glass window, this church has a huge window of 35 panes which dominates the building.

Sometimes it is possible for architects to take advantage of natural formations in the landscape to build structures of various kinds. The striking photograph below pictures the Red Rock Theater near Denver, Colorado.   This giant amphitheater was built be-

Red Rock Theater, near Denver, Colorado. Built on a natural hillside between two huge rock formations, this amphitheater is an excellent combination of natural beauty and man's ingenuity.

COURTESY, DEPARTMENT OF PARKS AND RECREATION,
CITY AND COUNTY OF DENVER

tween two huge natural rock walls, and faces a natural rock "sounding board." These undisturbed natural formations provide excellent acoustic properties. The huge rocks on either side are beautiful red sandstone. The sounding board at the back of the stage and most of the other rock outcroppings in the area are the same color. A large part of the construction was done with stone cut from the same material. There are seventy rows of seats on this hillside. Stretched end to end, they would reach nearly 2½ miles! The stage is 60 feet deep and 100 feet wide. What an impressive sight it is!

EXPERIENCES IN APPRECIATION

1. Select a style of architecture which was used in the period of history which you are studying. Ask your history teacher's coöperation in studying the life of the period. Try to find out why buildings were built as they were.

2. Arrange a "Know Your Architecture Contest." Your teacher will hang twenty pictures of buildings you do not know on the bulletin board. Each will bear a number. On your papers write the style of Architecture of each building.

3. Arrange a "Know Your Own Buildings Contest." A committee will collect pictures of local buildings. Each will be numbered. Write the name of the building and its style if it is one of the historic styles you have studied.

4. Arrange excursions to see the finest architecture in your community.

5. Prepare a report on your favorite style of architecture. Tell why it is your favorite, if possible. Show your collection of pictures.

6. Plan some criticism lessons on the architecture in your community. Remember that criticism includes good as well as bad comments.

7. List the places where the three Greek styles of columns are used in your community.

CREATIVE ACTIVITIES

1. Design the façade of a building in your favorite style.
2. Sketch the building in your community which you think is the best.
3. Model a gargoyle.

11

ART BEGINS AT HOME

A *SEARCH FOR* beauty may lead us to many places. For those who have learned to see it, there is beauty in the forest, the sky and the sea, in art galleries and public parks, in shops, theaters, and schools. *But our search for beauty should really begin at home.* It is here that we have our most frequent opportunities to enjoy beauty and to create it. Bits of beauty in our own rooms may mean much more to us than the great masterpieces of art in all the world's galleries. A nice arrangement of pictures, vases, and candlesticks on the mantel is something that can give us pleasure every day. An attractive table can please our eyes as well as our appetites at every meal. A lovely lamp, a fine rug, or pleasing draperies can bring us continued satisfaction as we go about our daily routine.

Remember, too, that each one of us becomes an artist when we buy the furnishings for our homes and arrange them according to our own tastes. Some of us are poor artists and some are good. Whether we manage to create attractive homes or not, depends on whether we have learned the rules for beauty and how to use these rules. We cannot expect to learn all about home decoration in one chapter, but what we have already learned in the preceding chapters will help us to deal with this art problem.

223

Arrangements—Large and Small

No matter how beautiful your furniture, lamps, rugs, walls, pictures, and vases, your home will not really be attractive and comfortable to live in unless these furnishings are arranged to the best advantage. If the mantel, sideboard, and dresser tops are loaded with articles shoved together in a helter-skelter arrangement, some of these objects, although beautiful, may lose their attractiveness. If the furniture is placed as though it were being shown off in a show window instead of for use in a home, it will lose its charm. If the pictures are hung on a skyline instead of your eyeline, and if flowers are jammed into vases instead of carefully arranged, the effect will be bad.

Remember that good arrangement does not require the expenditure of money. Generally it means making the best of what you have. Whether the furnishings are beautiful or ugly, they will appear better if properly arranged. Let us see how you tackle this problem of good arrangement.

Beautiful Flower Arrangements

A bouquet of beautiful flowers deserves a good arrangement. It is not right to pick flowers that are lovely in the garden or the woods, bring them into the house, and stuff them carelessly into ugly vases. If you do not care enough about them to arrange them nicely, leave them where they grow. Besides, arranging flowers in pleasing effects is a most enjoyable and interesting hobby. Many people get a great deal of fun out of it. Here is another chance to be an artist without use of brush or paint.

Below are some rules and suggestions which are useful in securing good flower arrangements. As you study each of these suggestions turn to the flower arrangements in the accompanying illustrations, and see how they were carried out.

The handsome, modern church above is located on the campus of the University of Connecticut at Storrs, Connecticut. It is a fine example of simplicity in modern architecture. Many modern churches are built without spires or tall bell towers, which are used on some churches to make them reach high. Instead, the verticals are emphasized, just as the architect did on the church pictured here. The apparent height has been increased by using long, thin vertical supports, and by tapering the building so that it is narrower at the top. This produces an illusion of greatly increased height when one stands near the church and looks up toward the cross.

1. Always choose a container that will not attract too much attention. Remember that the flowers are the center of interest. If the vase is too brightly colored or too much ornamented it will draw attention away from the flowers.

2. Select a container or cut the stems of the flowers so that the height of the bouquet is about once and a half the height of the container; or, if a low container is used, once and a half times the width of the container. This rule is based upon the art principle of proportion. Think of the whole arrangement as a design. The relation of proportions between the flowers and container should be about three to two. This does not mean that the topmost tip of the flower or leaves must be exactly once and a half as high as the container. The effect may be best if the tip is somewhat higher or lower. See Figures 124 and 125. Perhaps

In these arrangements the flowers are well proportioned to the vases.

FIGURE 124   FIGURE 125

COURTESY, MRS. DAVID R. KELLOGG

the rule really means avoid extreme proportions which are un-pleasant. For example, very tall flowers stuck in a low vase or short-stemmed flowers perched in the top of a tall vase are not good.

3. Avoid crossed stems. Crossed lines generally make ugly angles. On what principle of art is this rule based?

4. Arrange the heaviest and thickest part of the composition near the base of the stems. This gives a feeling of strength and support, or in other words good balance. See Figures 124 and 125.

5. When combining two or more kinds of flowers, or two or more colors in the same arrangement, plan to use more of one than another. If used in equal amounts, the effect is likely to be monotonous. What principle of art suggests this rule?

6. Balance the two sides of your flower arrangement. Informal balance is most generally used by experts in flower arrangements. Remember that in informal balance a larger and heavier mass nearer the center balances a lighter mass farther from the center. Can you see how this is managed in Figure 125? In 126? Formal balance is sometimes successfully used in flower arrangements, but the effect is likely to be more formal and elegant than we care for in our homes. There is also a tendency for formal flower ar-rangements to be stiff, though not if skillfully done.

7. Avoid stems of equal lengths. Cut them to get variety of spacing. See how this was accomplished in Figure 124. Also avoid stair-step effects.

8. Use buds, half-opened, and fully opened blossoms in the same arrangement when possible. This adds variety of form and size. See Figure 125.

9. Always think of the flowers and the container as parts of one design or composition. As you put the flowers into the vase try to make them look as though they belonged to each other. If

FIGURE 126. *An arrangement of berries and dried twigs in a glass container.*

the container is vertical in shape it will be best to arrange the flowers to suggest a vertical feeling. See Figure 125. Often it is helpful to place some flowers or foliage so that the edge of the container is partially concealed. See Figure 125. How are the containers and the plant materials blended together in each of the arrangements in Figure 126? In Figure 127?

FIGURE 127. An arrangement of a locust branch with still life objects. Notice the fine circular rhythms in the branch, tray, shells, and Buddha.

10. Use any plant materials for your flower arrangement which are at hand. There are any number of common plants, tree branches, vines, and berries than can be used with great success. Pussy willow, barberry, chestnut, locust branches, bittersweet, rose vines, mountain ash, and sumac are examples of common materials that may make charming arrangements. Even weeds can be used effectively. Thistles, dandelions, red clover, milkweed pods, mullen, and teasels are examples of weeds with good possibilities for artistic arrangements. Notice the arrangement with dried materials and branches in Figures 126 and 127.

11. Always plan your flower arrangement for a particular place. The effect of many a good bouquet has been ruined because it was placed upon a table already crowded or upon a bookcase with other objects that did not harmonize. If a flower arrangement is placed upon a table or bookcase it should have room to show off, and should harmonize with its surroundings. This may mean that you will have to remove a vase or other object so the flower arrangement will fit into the whole effect.

Necessary Equipment for Flower Arrangements

Tools and equipment are necessary for almost any hobby that you might choose. There is hardly any hobby that you might select which requires less equipment than flower arrangement. Of course, you will need plant materials and containers but these need not be expensive. Your tools are very simple—scissors, some thin wire or string to bind stems together, and some flower holders. The holders are very important. Without them you cannot keep the flowers and foliage in the proper places. Holders made in various styles can be purchased at the dime stores. There are glass blocks with holes, pin-point holders on which you press the stems, wire-mesh, bird-cage holders, and flexible wire holders. Of these types, the glass block is the least useful because it does not allow enough variation in the placing of the flowers. There are various homemade holders which are very useful. A ball of crumpled chicken wire pushed into a tall vase makes a very good holder. Sand in the bottom of a small container or cuttings from evergreens in an upright container are good holders.

Plan some day at school for practice on flower arrangements. Bring your own materials, and be sure to give careful thought to the problem.

Arrangement of the Pictures on Your Wall

Another problem in arrangement is the placing of pictures. Correct placing of pictures on our walls has a great deal to do with the attractive and comfortable effect that we desire. Below are some rules and suggestions that are helpful when you are hanging your pictures.

1. Pictures should be placed somewhere near the eye level. Never "sky" them. Since pictures are meant to be looked at, it is only reasonable to place them so it is easy to see them. No one wants to look at a picture hung near the ceiling.

2. Never hang a picture with a wire that shows unless absolutely necessary. Very large, heavy pictures may require wires from a molding. In this case two vertical wires should be used, never one wire which forms a triangle on top of the picture. These triangular wires have a confusing and distracting effect. After all, it is the pictures we are supposed to look at, not wires.

3. Avoid stair-step arrangements. It makes a scattered effect as though the pictures were about to fly away. It lacks unity.

4. Pictures should be placed when possible so as to become part of a group. For example, a picture hung over a piece of furniture makes it "belong" to that piece of furniture.

5. It is not necessary to hang *all* the pictures that you possess at the same time. If you have too many to hang them all with pleasing effect, save some of them until you wish to have a change.

6. Several small pictures can be hung effectively in a group. This is better than scattering them about in a hit-or-miss fashion. There are many ways in which pictures can be grouped. When you combine pictures of different sizes remember our rule for good proportions. Two tiny pictures on either side of one very large picture will not combine harmoniously because the difference in spaces is too great.

Several pictures hung near together should *look as though they belong together.* Think of the group as a panel and try to get a unified effect. This means that the pictures cannot be hung too far apart or they will not form a pleasing unit. On the other hand they should not be hung so close together that they detract from each other. The best thing to do when you are planning to hang some pictures in a group is to "try it on the eye." Try different arrangements until you find the one that seems best. Sometimes this can be done most easily by laying the pictures on a big table or on the floor. Then you can shift them about without driving tacks or nails into the wall.

Here are some suggestions for different arrangements which you might wish to try: two or more pictures in a horizontal row above the davenport; two or three pictures in a vertical row above the radio or television set; six pictures in a panel of two deep and three wide above your bed.

7. Pictures should be hung so they are flat against the wall, not tilted forward at the top.

Let each member of the class tell how he or she might improve the placing of the pictures in his or her own room. Explain with the aid of diagrams if you can.

Consider the Arrangement of a Wall

Good effects in small arrangements of articles on tops of mantels and chest, in bouquets, and in hanging of pictures are important, but good effects are perhaps even more important in larger arrangements such as the grouping of furniture against a wall. The same general rules can be used in making larger arrangements as in small arrangements. We want an effect of harmony, balance, pleasing proportions, rhythmic movement, and emphasis.

FIGURE 128. A pleasing arrangement of furniture and accessories in a wall space between two windows.

The arrangement in the wall space between two windows shown in Figure 128 is unified and pleasing. In this case identical objects have been used on either side of the center, thus producing formal balance. The chairs and chest are in good proportion to each other, creating a feeling of harmonious relationships. This type of arrangement is often used in a dining room with the buffet in the center, or in the living room with the fireplace centered.

The view of the fireplace wall in Figure 129 shows an interesting modern arrangement. The fireplace is not centered as in the traditional style, but is placed toward the left-hand side. The large picture is nearer to the center of the mantel than the small pottery bowls to the right. Further weight is added to the right-

232

hand side by the arrangement of dark tree branches standing in the corner of the room. Does it seem strange to you that these bare tree branches should be brought into the house for this purpose? Well, why not use them if they add charm and interest to the room? Remember our study of tree branches in winter in Chapter 4. Is it not a good idea to bring some of this outdoor beauty inside? Of course, you may not always have the right place for such large arrangement, but a smaller arrangement on the mantel might be just the thing for some indoor beauty from winter trees.

Notice the emphasis on horizontal lines in the design of this modern living room. The long, low line of the mantel is echoed in the chairs and coffee table. These low, horizontal lines are characteristic of the modern style in furnishing and building.

FIGURE 129. A modern room expressing informal balance.

Beauty for Breakfast, Lunch, and Dinner

You can eat with art at every meal if you think about it when you select your china, silver, and tablecloths, and if you take pains with setting the table attractively. Every dish, spoon, and place mat is a possible bit of beauty. It does not matter whether they come from the dime store or the most exclusive shop in town— they can be beautiful at any price. Why should we not enjoy a bit of beauty with our breakfast cereal and our pork chops, when it can be had at the same cost?

Decoration Should Beautify

Much of the china that we use on our tables is decorated with bands of color, floral patterns, or other motifs. The designers who create this decoration mean to make the china more beautiful, but because they sometimes do not know the rules for decoration, they make it more ugly.

Floral patterns are used a great deal for the decoration of table china. No doubt you have many times eaten from dishes decorated with flowers and leaves. The decoration on the English bone china shown in Figure 130 is a nice example of one kind of floral decoration. The leaves are designed in bands which conform very harmoniously with the shape of the china. Notice that the bands of decoration are placed so that they harmonize with the structure of the piece. Some people say that this kind of decoration is "too set." Isn't it as pleasing as realistic sprays of flowers scattered accidentally over the dishes? This type of decoration is orderly and well organized. Some people like it much better than decoration than spreads across the dishes in an informal fashion. It looks as though it were meant to fit the dishes it decorates.

Those who like a more informal pattern will be pleased with

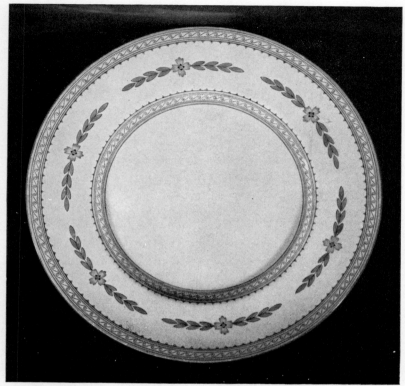

*FIGURE 130. Pleasing decoration of floral bands, a type which is formal
in character.*

the china in Figure 131. Units with a floral motif decorate the
center of the plate, the tops of the sugar bowl and teapot, and the
insides of the cream pitcher and teacup. Yet these are "design
flowers." We have no feeling that they are real flowers painted
on the china. The effect is very gay and charming. This kind of
decoration is sometimes called free decoration because the original
design was made with free brush strokes. We like it for the free,
swinging strokes in each leaf, stem, and petal.

FIGURE 131. Informal floral decorations used with charming effect.

Pictures or Designs on Our China?

Everyone likes fine pictures, but not everyone likes them painted on his dinner dishes. Suppose you like dog pictures. Would you like to find a very real picture of a collie under your meat and potatoes every night? It hardly seems suitable to place your food on a collie's face! A realistic picture may look very well hung on the wall, but it is out of place on our table china. We prefer to have our dishes decorated with designs and not pictures. Very amusing and interesting decorations can be made from flowers, dogs, and even the human form, but we do not want them to suggest reality. The very idea of putting food on top of a picture is unpleasant.

Collect pictures of dishes and vases with floral decorations. How many have the appearance of fitting the structural form? How many decorations look as though they were accidentally dropped on the dishes?

From your collection of pottery examples select those which you think suggest too much realism. Then select those which are properly decorative.

Loveliness in Glass

No article for table use can furnish greater beauty than glassware. Glass goblets, plates, and other pieces add lustrous, sparkling beauty to the dinner hour. Fine contours, the shining loveliness of clear glass, and the exciting tones of colored glass each deserves special notice.

The goblet shown in Figure 132 has a very fine contour. The beautiful sweeping curve from stem to rim and the spreading shape of the base create a most delightful effect. The clear, crystal-like texture adds to the charm of the goblet. This is the sort of everyday article that can give you joy every time you see it.

The table setting in Figure 133 appeals to everyone because it is so splendidly designed. Had you thought of a table setting as a design? This is something to remember when you set the table for dinner and perhaps the job will seem a bit less dull. Instead of using paint and brush, you can do your designing with place

FIGURE 132. A goblet illustrating a very fine contour.

238

FIGURE 133.   Beautiful table setting in glass.

mats, dishes, silver, and a centerpiece. In Figure 133 the linen place mats create a rectangular pattern on the dark, polished wood, and the knives, forks and spoons echo the rectangular shapes. Is it not fortunate that rules for placing the silver do not create an inharmonious effect? The circular shapes of the glass dishes produce a charming contrast with the rectangular pattern. The centerpiece makes an interesting center of interest. Although it may seem rather high for conversation across the table, this is due to the way the camera was focused.

We Eat in Style!

There are literally hundreds of designs for silverware alone! We eat in style! Have you ever considered how advantageous it is to select any pattern you want? Many families have two, even three sets of tableware. Do you use a different set for just "every day," and another for special occasions? Perhaps your family is like many others, with a set of stainless steel and another of silver.

FIGURE 134. *A contemporary silver design with simple lines and smooth surfaces.*

COURTESY, GEORG JENSEN

FIGURE 135. Two silver designs in the elegant style. Their rich, sculptured surfaces contrast sharply with the simplicity of contemporary silver.

The photograph on the preceding page shows a fine example of contemporary silver design. Contemporary design means that which is being done now. Notice the smooth, flowing line of this silver. There are no ornaments to break its satin-smooth surface. This silver would look well with many styles of china because its simple shape would not be out of place. Some silver designs are made to look elegant, and should be used with china and other table accessories that are also elegant. The sterling silver patterns pictured above would help to "dress up" any dinner table. They are fine examples of the silversmithing art. The first is a simple shape with a flower motif. This pattern might be considered more versatile than the lower one. That is, it might be used for a greater variety of table settings. The lower pattern is a traditional floral and leaf design. It has a rich, finely detailed quality unlike most contemporary pieces. Whether you live casually or formally, you will find a silver pattern to suit your taste.

Fine designs in silver are not limited to knives, forks, and spoons. For many years craftsmen have excelled in creating bowls, pitchers, trays, and other beautiful serving pieces to grace the tables in our homes. Often these craftsmen enter their work in competition, or sell the pieces to discriminating people who want the best. A young American craftsman, Alfred H. Wardle, has created the silver pitcher below, and the handsome silver service on the next page. He hammered these beautiful shapes from flat pieces of silver. Notice that the handles are wrapped with

FIGURE 136. A handcrafted silver pitcher with beautiful functional shape.

COURTESY, ALFRED H. WARDLE

FIGURE 137. Matching silver service, hammered from flat pieces of silver.

flat reed. This material acts as an insulator besides adding interest to the designs. That coffee server would be too hot to hold without it! The proportion of the handles to the pitchers is pleasing. These silver designs can be called functional, since they were created primarily for use, not for appearance. However, Wardle has combined the principles of function with good taste. For example, he has bent the handles so that the pitchers may be easily tipped for pouring. The reed wrapping is also a functional addition. Yet both the handles and the wrapping enhance the general appearance.

FIGURE 138. A set of teakwood salad bowls from Denmark.

Wood has always been a favorite material for making bowls and other table accessories. The set of salad bowls shown here, designed by Finn Juhl of Denmark, is a beautiful example of fine craftsmanship coupled with good design. The most interesting characteristic is the graceful dip in the sides of the bowls. This gives them an interesting contour from any angle, and at the same time provides a place to rest the serving spoon and fork. Isn't this another good example of functional art?

For the Center of the Table

The center of the table needs a decoration, both during meals and between meals. It can be very simple and inexpensive, yet create a pleasing center of interest. A tray or bowl filled with fruits or vegetables makes a good decoration, especially in the autumn. Garden flowers provide material for very attractive table decorations. The pretty arrangement in Figure 139 was made

FIGURE 139. A delightful arrangement of garden chrysanthemums and juniper suitable for a dining table.

from small branches of juniper and garden chrysanthemums. It was designed for a long table and fills the requirement admirably. Note the graceful swing of the juniper branches and the cluster of blossoms which form a center of interest for the bouquet.

Decorative Accessories Can Be Beautiful

Everyone likes the extra things which give a room the look of being "dressed up" and well decorated. Pictures on the walls, vases, ceramic figures, and clocks, all add to the general effect, and, of course, you want the general effect to be beautiful. Choose these small articles with care, lest you add ugliness instead of beauty to your room. Design and color are important in every object, even though it be very small. Look at the decorative ceramic fish in Figure 140. He is an impudent little fish and seems to be telling some rude fisherman just what he thinks of him!

FIGURE 140.   A gay and amusing ceramic fish.

COURTESY, JOSEPH C. FITZPATRICK

FIGURE 141. A beautiful vase-pitcher designed and created by Frances Serber and William Soini.

The vase-pitcher shown in Figure 141 has a modern design of unusual beauty. The fine contour is enhanced by the splendid curve of the handle and the forward thrust of the spout. It can be used for holding long-stemmed flowers or branches from flowering shrubs. Even when not used as a flower container, it is an especially beautiful decorative accessory.

FIGURE 142. In this interesting ceramic figure Richard Davis has created his interpretation of Washington Irving's famous schoolmaster.

The ceramic figures in Figures 142 and 143 are interesting interpretations of two characters in American folklore, one fictional and one real. The first is Ichabod Crane, from *The Legend of Sleepy Hollow* by Washington Irving, written a little more than a century ago. Ichabod was the schoolmaster of Sleepy Hollow who courted the daughter of the wealthiest man in the community. As he rode home the dark night just after he had been rejected by the lady of his dreams, he was frightened by the Headless Horseman who carried his head upon the pommel of his saddle! Poor Ichabod tried to escape but just as he neared safety, the Headless Horseman hurled his "head," knocking Ichabod from his saddle. The schoolmaster was never again seen in those parts. Next

FIGURE 143. "Johnny Appleseed," by Nathaniel Kaz, is an interesting interpretation of the famous character of frontier days.

morning his horse was found riderless, and nearby Ichabod's hat and a shattered pumpkin.

Ichabod was described in the story as "tall, but exceedingly lank, with narrow shoulders, long arms and legs, hands that dangled a mile out of his sleeves, feet that might have served as shovels, and his whole frame most loosely hung together." The author also mentions his "spindle neck" and small head. If you have not already read the story, you will find it amusing. You might find it worth while to read the story again.

The interpretation of Ichabod Crane by Richard Davis is really a caricature, yet is beautiful in line and form. Note the small head, long arms and legs, and the book which is a symbol of his occupation.

The ceramic figure shown opposite Ichabod Crane is Johnny Appleseed, an American frontier hero. His real name was John Chapman and he lived near Pittsburgh Landing more than a century ago. Here he developed a large nursery where he sold or gave apple seeds and saplings to families that were migrating westward. He collected seeds from cider presses, dried them, and put them into small bags which he urged on the frontier people. Later he made many trips by canoe down the Ohio and on foot through Ohio, Indiana, and Illinois carrying his sacks of apple seeds to settlers in this region. As a result, hundreds of orchards grew where Johnny Appleseed had traveled through the country. Many legends grew also, stories of his help and kindness to the settlers and families who were in danger. There are also many stories of his heroism in the War of 1812, among them the story of how he saved Mansfield, Ohio, from an Indian attack. He is buried in a cemetery near Fort Wayne, Indiana.

In the ceramic figure shown on page 251, the artist, Nathaniel Kaz, has created this strange, emaciated figure with his bag of apple seeds in his left hand and using his right hand to press down the soil as he plants an apple seed.

Do you ever think of Johnny Appleseed as you pass by an apple orchard? Or eat a luscious apple?

Lamps Have Gone Modern

Designs for lamps, along with furniture and many other furnishings, are now in the modern style. Designs in the past have included imitation candlesticks and oil lamps, and lampshade decorations of lace, fringe, artificial flowers, and swirling silk drapes! Aren't you glad you live in a modern age?

A. DESIGNED BY ZAHARA SCHATZ,
HEIFETZ MANUFACTURING COMPANY

B. DESIGNED BY ROBSJOHN-GIBBINGS,
THE WIDDICOMB FURNITURE COMPANY

*FIGURE 144. Three modern lamp designs.
A. A single bent tube is curved to form the
lamp base and to support the light cone and
reflector. B. Three metal rods form the base
and also support the shade. C. A lamp
which can be adjusted for study, reading, or
general illumination. Lamps A and C received awards in a contest sponsored by the
Museum of Modern Art.*

C. DESIGNED BY JOHN VAN ZWEINEN,
HEIFETZ MANUFACTURING COMPANY

The lamps in Figure 144 are designed for electric bulbs and wires. In no way are they imitations of candlesticks or oil lamps. In Lamp A the light bulb is contained in the cone which is pointed upward, throwing the light against the reflector above. This cone or urn can be rotated in different directions. The reflector can be tipped in any direction or at any angle. With this flexibility, a number of different lighting adjustments can be made.

In Design B, we find a complete change from the traditional type of base. Here the wire runs up inside one leg of the tripod base and the shade rests on the tips of the same metal rods which form the base.

In Design C there is great flexibility in controlling the light. The handle can be tipped to raise or lower the light and also rotated as desired. The shade is white translucent parchment, and the base is solid African mahogany.

Collect pictures of lamp designs and discuss them for simplicity, beauty, suitability to electricity, and ease with which light can be adjusted to different purposes.

Beauty Rules for Furniture

Good design in furniture depends on the same art principles with which we have become familiar. Let us see how they apply to the selection of various pieces of furniture. Begin with the davenports in Figure 145. The first one is the type known as a Lawson davenport. It has graceful lines and pleasing proportions. This design is much more beautiful than some of the great, heavy, overstuffed davenports that cost more money. Some modern davenports look like several mattresses bunched together! They have no lines! It is not necessary for comfort or beauty to have davenport arms stuffed to colossal proportions. A davenport is bound to be a large and heavy piece of furniture, but it need be

FIGURE 145. *A Lawson davenport with graceful lines and pleasing pro-*
portions. Contrast this clean-cut design with some of the very heavy-look-
ing, bulky davenports that are really "overstuffed."

FIGURE 146. *A more modern design in a davenport. This one is simple*
in design and will fit into casual arrangements as easily as formal ones.

253

no more ponderous than necessary for comfort. Bulky davenports
and chairs are too large for many living rooms.

The second davenport in Figure 145 is also pleasing in line and
proportion. The arms and legs are graceful and strong. The up-
holstering material is well suited to this type of davenport.

There is a beautiful, cretonne-covered chair in Figure 146. The
lines are pleasing, the proportions are nice, and the pattern of the
cretonne is very decorative. The other chair also has a good design. Notice how the curves of the arms flow into the back of the
chair. Does this make you think of the way the handle of a teacup blends into the contour of the whole cup? The legs echo the
curved lines in the upper part of the chair. The styling is fresh
and sturdy.

Perhaps you prefer straight lines in chair designs. The chairs
and most of the other furniture in Figure 147 are in straight lines.
This furniture is plain and simple in effect. It is also sturdy and
strong. This room is called a boy's room but there is no reason
why it should not be a girl's room. Many girls prefer this simple,
sturdy-looking furniture.

Now compare the two chests in Figures 146 and 147. The first
is more elegant and luxurious in effect than the other. This quality is secured chiefly by the fancy, metal drawer pulls and by the
curved pieces on the legs. The other chest has only plain wooden
pulls and a very simple base. This does not prove that one chest
is more beautiful than the other. Both are very good looking, and
either one you might choose is a good selection.

Perhaps when you choose your furniture you will wish to have
the modern style. Page 258 shows a collection of modern chairs.
Like the silver service and davenport, page 255, these are also
contemporary pieces. Chairs A and B are small, and light in
weight. They would serve well in the dining room, or perhaps

PHOTOGRAPH BY HOLMES I. METTEE, COURTESY, W. T. WHITNEY COMPANY

FIGURE 147. *A group of fine furniture near an interesting window.*

COURTESY, PARENTS MAGAZINE AND W. T. WHITNEY COMPANY

FIGURE 148. *A boy's room furnished in a simple, sturdy style*

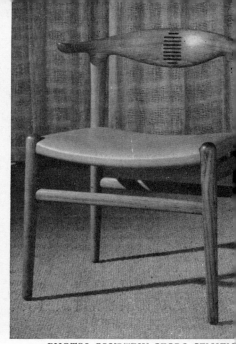

A. Lightweight chair with cane seat,
molded arms.

B. Lightweight, curved-back chair
with leather seat.

C. Upholstered chair with curved
arms, unique supports.

D. Cane-woven seat for dressing
table or "extra" chair. Notice the
convenient carrying handles.

FIGURE 149.   *A collection of contemporary chairs.*

The picture above shows a very impressive living room furnished in traditional style. The eye is first attracted to the davenport and the decorative arrangement above. The location of the sofa between two matching tables and lamps, with identical red chairs on either side, creates a most pleasing formal arrangement. The narrow shelf just above the davenport, the arrangement of flowers, books, and pewter shown against the dark green color, add interest and glamor to the effect. Is there something familiar about the book ends?

The arrangement of the furniture invites one to come and enjoy a pleasant hour. The sofa actually serves a dual purpose—at night it can be opened to make a comfortable bed. The color scheme is worked out in tones of green, yellow, and red. Notice the agreeable textured quality of the rug, davenport, and chairs. You might enjoy making up color names for these fabrics—cherry red, mossy green, dull gold.

256A

The beautiful living room above, designed in contemporary or modern style, impresses us with its feeling of space and rich inventiveness. The effect is produced chiefly by the use of long, low lines, different textures, and simplicity of color.

The line formed by the long, black fireplace ledge is important in creating the dramatic effect. The fireplace is raised from the floor, and the ledge serves as the hearth as well as a seat extending the length of the wall. Since the hearth would have to be fireproof, the ledge might be made of black marble or perhaps of concrete painted black. The rectangular lines of the fireplace are repeated by the lines of the sofa and the long, low table in front of it. The vertical lines of the modern fold door and the horizontal book shelves fit nicely into the over-all design of the room.

The color harmony is simple, but has been planned in excellent taste. The off-white areas of wall and floor make a counterpoint for the smaller areas of black and red. Observe that there is no ornamentation—only plain surfaces. This is another way in which the modern designer secures an effect of spaciousness.

as extra chairs for the living room or den. We can see that they were designed for easy carrying. They're light in weight as mentioned, but, more important, they are strongly constructed. This is a good point to remember when you must purchase a chair one day. You'll want a strong one, light enough so that you can grasp the back and carry it quickly from one room to another. How many chairs in your home can you lift and carry in this manner? An up-to-date home needs something just like this, don't you agree?

Chair C is a "lightweight" too, but it's not the kind we carry from place to place. It's light enough to move for easy cleaning of the rug, but too big to move about freely. The most interesting characteristic of this neat-looking design is the method of construction and bracing. Wouldn't it be easy to clean under it? Have you ever seen a full-sized chair with this much room underneath?

That last photograph, D, is our special pet. Here we must use that word function again! Remember what it means? This seat is designed to do a specific job, in the best possible way. A quick glance tells us that we have just what we need for an extra light, comfortable chair-for-anywhere. Want to move it? Just pick it up by the handles and take it away!

The appearances of all these chairs have something in common. What do you think it is? Your answer should state that they're all simple in design, and beautifully molded. Of course you might not say it in that way, but you should be aware of both of those points. There's a good reason for this combination, and you should remember it for the future. The beauty of wood is in the grain and finish of the surface. The designers of contemporary furniture take their cue from hand craftsmen who have known this for years! All the chairs you see on page 256 are carefully designed to show off the beauty of the wood.   Rounded surfaces and graceful joinery complement the satiny finish.

There Are Two Sides to Every Story!

How often have you heard someone say, "There are two sides to every story"?   We're a complex people.   Every time a new-style car, a changed hemline, or a speedier bicycle is made, someone will say, "That's the *only* thing to have.   The rest of you are old-fashioned!"   Well, this has been going on since John Caveman told his father that times had changed, and that he should get with the rest of the crowd.   But John's father was like some of us. He had a few things around the cave that *his* father had used, and he liked them.   Not only that, he planned to make a few more exactly like those he had and give them to his relatives.   Of course you know what John's father was up to.   He intended to convince as many people as he could that the new generation had developed some ideas that were simply ridiculous.   Imagine using wood for furniture when the whole house was full of rock benches!   There were some folks who agreed, and they continued to enjoy living in the traditional way.   John's ideas were sound, too.   "Why not try something new?" he asked.   "Look.   I can carry my stool!" His might have been the first contemporary style, since it developed in the same way as ours.   You can be certain this tale has no basis in historical fact, but it does serve to point out that both John and his father had sound notions.

Fortunately, we're not in the predicament that both John and his father were.   Most of our furniture is comfortable, but none of theirs was, by our standards.   So if we are to decide for ourselves whether we prefer traditional or contemporary styling, our choice will depend primarily on appearance, with a great deal of inside help from our personalities.   See pages 256A,B.

FIGURE 150. Colonial house in Williamsburg, Virginia.

Art Outside Your House

Beauty of a house exterior depends on good design, just as does any article of furnishing inside the house. The pictures in Figures 150 and 151 show two very different styles of architecture—both beautiful. The first is an old Colonial house in Williamsburg, Virginia, and the other is a modern style house in Minneapolis, Minnesota. Characteristics of the Colonial house are a steep pitched roof, small square windowpanes, shutters, white clapboard, and red brick chimneys. A pleasing rhythm of triangular

259

FIGURE 151. *A modern style house in Minnesota.*

lines and shapes is created by the roof, the tops of the dormer windows, and the broadened base of the chimney.

The modern house in Figure 151 is quite different in design. The roof is almost flat but has a slight pitch which allows the snow to slide over the edge. It is characterized by the nearly flat roof, the window walls on both the upper and lower levels, the redwood siding and the broad brick chimney, and emphasis on horizontal lines.

Another style which has become very popular in recent years

FIGURE 152. *The ranch type house has become very popular.*

FIGURE 153. *The street view of "the house that borrowed from nature"*
shows the carport and the walk leading to the entrance by the plant box.

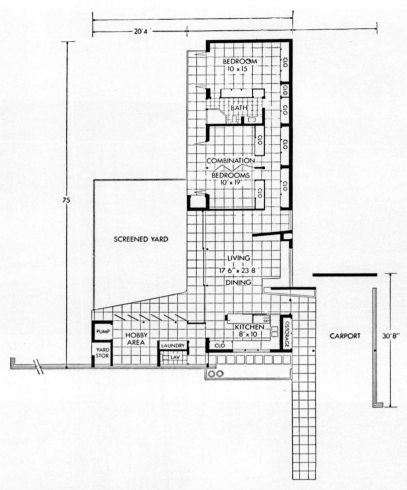

FIGURE 154. The floor plan of the house, Fig. 153. Trace your path as you enter by the plant box and walk through the rooms. Note the glass walls and screened yard.

is shown in Figure 152—the ranch-type house. It is a low, one-story house with the roof extending out over the porch. Windows and doors are arranged so as to create an effect of informal balance. The low-pitched roof and the long lines of the house and porch create a charming picture.

FIGURE 155. This is the carport and shows the open entrance door just to the left of the plant box. The large wood doors conceal a storage area.

There are many styles of houses and perhaps one of these three is not your favorite. However, you should be able to enjoy good design in houses wherever you see them, even though you prefer one special style.

A Modern House—Inside and Out

The modern house shown in Figures 153, 154, 155 and 156 is called "the house that borrowed from nature," meaning that it brings the outdoors inside and the indoors outside. Study the floor plan and you will see that the glass walls swing or slide open into the screened yard. The bedrooms also open to the outside, thus

FIGURE 156. *The living and dining areas are combined in one room. (See the floor plan.) The plant box is continued inside the glass wall.*

providing easy access to the yard and allowing plenty of light and air to enter the inside.

The picture at the top left, Figure 153, shows a view of the house looking into the carport, and the floor plan below, Figure 154, shows how you can walk along beside the carport and turn into the living-dining area. Or you can turn into the walk along the front of the house and enter another door. The picture at the top right, Figure 155, shows the carport without its car. Here you can see the outside part of the plant box. In the next picture (Figure 156), you can see how the plant box is continued inside the glass wall so as to give a continuous effect of planting.

A House That Fits the Ground

We've talked about a house that fits people, but we've said nothing about its appearance from the street. Does it fit the ground? Just as certain kinds of furniture fit you, so should the house fit the ground. It should look as if it belongs where it is. In order to make houses seem a part of the landscape, some architects design their houses to suit the slope, and to go with the characteristics of the trees and shrubs that are there. The house below is an excellent example of a house that fits the site. The ground is nearly flat, so the house was designed to appear close to it, creating a horizontal, rather than vertical, movement. This was achieved by accenting the horizontal structural members, such as the roof and low front wall. On the other hand, the vertical lines were sub-

FIGURE 157. *A house that fits the ground.*

COURTESY, ALUMINUM COMPANY OF AMERICA

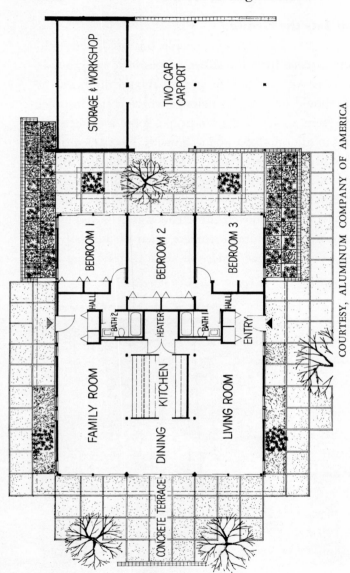

COURTESY, ALUMINUM COMPANY OF AMERICA

FIGURE 159. *The floor plan of this Alcoa "Care-Free Home" illustrates the simplicity of design which contributes to the dwelling's ease of maintenance. The family room, with its own entrance, provides a family gathering place and reserves the living room for formal entertaining. Baths are easily accessible from all parts of the home, and the master bedroom is strategically located in relation to the adjacent smaller bedrooms for children or guests.*

COURTESY, ALUMINUM COMPANY OF AMERICA

FIGURE 158. Garden area outside bedrooms. Plants grow all year round in this protected, sunny spot.

dued. To do this, the architect used metal columns in the front of the house. They are scarcely noticeable. The thin columns with lacy grillwork next to them repeat the growth pattern of the trees. The columns repeat the straight, thin verticals of the trunks, while the grillwork reflects the leaf pattern. The handsome high wall in front of the house also helps relate the house to the ground with its open, leaf-like design.

The photograph above shows the area behind the front wall. The roof is cut out to permit the sunlight to enter. Notice how the wall blends in with the leaf pattern. A look at the plan at right shows us that the large glass doors open from the bedrooms.

The general idea and plan of this modern house is very different from the traditional house. It has an "open" arrangement which is new in house design. At first it may seem strange, but as you get better acquainted with this type of architecture you will enjoy its beauty.

Design in Your Planting

The planting of flowers and shrubs around a house can help or harm its beauty. A house with no planting around its foundation seems bare and ugly. It does not seem to belong to the ground upon which it is built. A few shrubs and flowers close to the foundation help to relate the house to its grounds. Foundation planting should be planned to harmonize with the house and add interest to the whole effect. Notice in Figure 159 how the shrubs help to "tie" the house to the ground and add interest to the design. This is much more desirable than an even row of bushes straight around the house.

Planting Pictures in Your Garden

Anyone who wishes that he could paint beautiful pictures may realize his ambition in his garden. Instead of painting them he can plant them. Instead of paints he will use plant materials. Have you not heard someone exclaim over a lovely garden, "Isn't that a picture!" Anyone who plans and plants a beautiful garden can rightfully be called an artist.

Our study of sculptures and painting has shown us that the artist puts a great deal of thought and planning into his work. This is also true of the artist who creates a fine garden. He must design his garden so that the final effect will really be a picture.

Careful planning is even more important in the small garden

FIGURE 160. A pleasant, little retreat in a city backyard.

than in the large one. In the small garden a few inches is more important than a half acre on a large estate. Following are some beauty rules for the design of small gardens.

1. Boundaries are backgrounds. The edges of your garden are important. If you plant tall shrubs, their foliage will make a green background against which you see flowers and other objects in your garden. If you build a stone wall or fence, you will have a different background. If you do neither of these things, leaving the boundaries open, then the view beyond will form the

background.   If the surroundings are lovely you may wish to do this, but often we like to shut in our gardens, both for the sake of privacy as well as for a solid background.   Notice how shrubbery forms a background and secures privacy for the tiny garden in Figure 160.

2. Plan a center of interest for your garden.   One feature in every garden should be emphasized.   The center of interest may be a small pool, a rose trellis, a sundial, table and chairs, or a piece of garden sculpture.   What would you consider the center of interest in Figure 160?

3. Plan interesting spaces in your garden.   It is generally best in small gardens to leave the largest space for unbroken lawn. This gives the impression of a larger lawn than where the lawn is broken by paths or by round flower beds or shrubs set here and there in the center.   Compare the small gardens in Figures 160 and 161.   Which one gives the impression of more space? Why?

4. Remember that small spaces are very important in a small garden.   A little corner that is neglected and shabby may be made a charming spot.   The picture in Figure 163 shows how the small space around an old pump was made attractive.   The tiny pool was made by sinking an old tub in the ground.   Grass, forget-me-nots, and other plants were planted close to the edge of the tub. The result is very pleasing.   The same scheme could be carried out at the water faucet attached to the wall of a house or standing in the garden.

5. Plan the colors in your garden so they will harmonize.   The beauty of many a garden has been spoiled because colors were planted next to each other which were not pleasing.   Brilliant orange-red day lilies in front of delicate, pink, rambler roses is a most unhappy combination.   The delicacy of the pink roses is overwhelmed by the brilliance of the lilies.   Bright orange and

FIGURE 161. A small yard can become a delightful outdoor living area.

yellow marigolds planted next to pink hibiscus or pink chrysanthemums make another unfortunate combination. Blue-and-purple iris is better in front of the delicate, pink, rambler roses. Blue cornflowers are better near the pink chrysanthemums and the pink hibiscus. In general, the delicate pinks and blues do not harmonize well with the brilliant yellows and orange colors.

If you are planting flowers in front of a wall, think of their color as it will be seen with the wall as a background. Pink azaleas do not show off well in front of a yellow brick wall. Yellow or flame

271

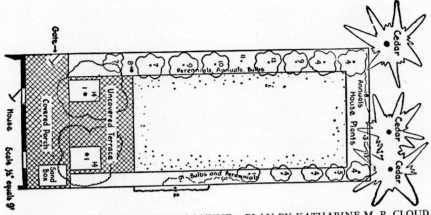

FIGURE 162. This plan for the garden on the previous page was made before the planting was done. The key given above tells what is planted in each part of the garden. 1, Lilac; 2, Privet; 3, 6 and 11, Climbing roses; 4, Forsythia; 5 and 7, Deutzia; 8, Hurricane lamp plunged in soil; 9, Weigela; 10, Hydrangea; 12, Spirea Anthony Waterer; 13, Ivy; 14, Pachysandra.

colored azaleas will be much more beautiful. If you have a red brick wall, blue and white flowers may be best. If the brick is very dark pink, pale yellow flowers may be successful.

The garden in Figure 161 is a delightful example of planting pictures in a small garden space. The view is taken from the edge of the uncovered terrace. You can see in the garden plan, Figure 162, that an uncovered terrace extends beyond the covered porch. As you study the key for the planting of shrubs, you will see that flowering shrubs which bloom at different times were chosen. First comes the forsythia with its brilliant yellow bloom in early spring, then the weigelia, lilac, deutzia, roses, and hydrangea to give the garden color as the season progresses. The family that planned and planted this garden literally live outdoors all summer.

FIGURE 163. A tiny pool at the foot of the garden pump.

In good weather they put up a card table on the uncovered terrace for outdoor meals; when it rains they move it to the covered porch which adjoins the kitchen.

Many Art Problems at Home

We have seen that there are dozens of art problems at home, both inside and outside. It is fun to work them out. Housework is more fun when you try to make interesting arrangements with your furnishings; shopping is more fun when you remember your beauty rules, and gardening is more exciting when you try for fine design and color harmony.

EXPERIENCES IN APPRECIATION

1. Make three diagrams showing three different arrangements for hanging pictures above a mantel; a sideboard; a bed.
2. Discuss the hanging of pictures in your school. How may the rules for hanging pictures in a school differ from those for hanging pictures in a home?
3. Arrange for a day when the class discussion is about beauty in weeds. Bring weeds to class. Try arranging them in suitable containers.

4. Collect pictures of lamps. Classify them into two groups, good and bad design.

5. Collect pictures to show the kind of furniture you would like to have for your own room. Plan the most beautiful room you can imagine.

6. Collect pictures of house exteriors and select the type that you like best.

7. Plan a garden for your home. Collect pictures to show how you would plant it.

8. Arrange a day when each member of the class will bring a dish to school. Hold a class criticism for design in china. Remember to include both structural and decorative design.

9. Plan a beautiful table for some special occasion such as Christmas, Easter, or a birthday. Illustrate it as well as you can with pictures. Explain your color scheme both in foods and in service equipment.

10. Collect pictures of wall arrangements, furniture, garden arrangements, houses, pieces of wallpaper, and any other material which can be discussed and criticized for art quality.

CREATIVE ACTIVITIES

1. Sketch flower arrangements in water color or crayon, with particular reference to art principles discussed in this chapter.

2. Design a lamp that you would like to have for your own room.

3. Design a striped awning for your own house. Remember to have an interesting arrangement of spaces and colors which harmonize with the color of your house.

4. Design a cretonne pattern for the curtains in your own room.

5. Design a hooked rug. Perhaps you can actually make the rug. In this case make your design on a large piece of wrapping paper and transfer the pattern to burlap.

6. Design the desk that you would like to have.

7. Design some wallpaper for your own room. Use water color or crayon. Remember that walls are a background.

8. Design a sugar bowl and cream pitcher.

9. Make a clay tile, applying what you know about the principles of good decorative design.

10. Make a floral centerpiece for a special occasion.

12

KEEP THE WORLD BEAUTIFUL

THIS IS a chapter with a moral. It "preaches" at you, and tells you what you should do. Perhaps you will not like it, but anyway it is a short chapter. It has just one idea, *your responsibility for keeping the world beautiful.*

We have found beauty in art galleries and in our homes, in the country and in the city, in man-made objects and in nature. Some of it like the great statues of Khephren and Abraham Lincoln are strong and lasting. Some beauty like that in many fine school buildings, is more easily spoiled. Here is where your responsibility comes in. If you mark on the walls, scratch your initials on the desks, and break down the shrubbery around the building, then you are making ugliness. We know that everyone likes his world to be beautiful, but not everyone helps to keep it that way. Would you not rather attend a school in a clean, attractive building with lawns, shrubs, and flower beds around it, than go to a dingy, unkept building surrounded with only bare ground? Certainly if you are fortunate enough to attend an attractive school, you should feel responsible for keeping it that way.

Here is a true story. A junior-high-school boy who was talented in art had carved a head from stone. His teacher asked him to bring it to school and show it to the class. It was a heavy thing to carry but he brought it, and also his tools. Before school he was showing it and his tools to some of his classmates. One of

275

them said, "How can you cut stone with a chisel?" The boy said, "I will show you." They were standing near a statue which decorated the front of the school building. With his chisel and hammer, the boy chipped a corner off the base of the statue!

This boy had created a head of some beauty from stone, but he failed to do his part in keeping his own school building beautiful. He did not deface the statue wilfully. He was thoughtless. Of course, this is no excuse for destroying beauty.

Some people purposely destroy the things which other people enjoy. The park superintendent of any great city will tell you that thousands of dollars worth of property are destroyed every year

FIGURE 164. *A realistic museum portrayal of a beautiful Pennsylvania vale in springtime.*

COURTESY, DEPARTMENT OF THE MUSEUM, CARNEGIE INSTITUTE

by people who think it is fun. Benches are tipped over and broken, windows are smashed, statues are smeared with paint, shrubs are broken, trees are killed by knife cuts in their trunks, and signs are spoiled. Parks are planned for the enjoyment of people who can not afford their own private parks, yet some of these same people destroy these parks. Can you explain it? What is wrong with these people? If you enjoyed a pleasant park and playground in your city, would you try to ruin it? It is very foolish to ruin the thing that can bring you some pleasure.

Most people do not go about deliberately spoiling the attractive things in their homes and communities. But many of them do

FIGURE 165. The same beautiful vale as in Figure 164—but after a picnic!

COURTESY, DEPARTMENT OF THE MUSEUM, CARNEGIE INSTITUTE

it through carelessness. Dirty fingermarks on the wallpaper or on the pages of a library book are careless. Throwing away school papers on the street is another kind of carelessness. Tramping across the corner of the lawn when the grass is young and the ground is soft is careless. If you value an attractive home and neighborhood, beware of carelessness!

Nearly everyone likes to go on picnics. It is fun to go out into the country and find a pleasant spot to eat lunch. Trees, skies, flowers, grass, and sunshine are splendid. The nicer the spot you can find, the more fun it is. Who could ask for a better place than the one shown in Figure 164? It was a lovely place in the Pennsylvania woods. Many people could have enjoyed a picnic lunch here, but some people came who did not care about its beauty. You can see in Figure 165 what happened after they had been there. Probably they did not destroy this natural beauty purposely. They were just thoughtless and careless.

Your responsibility for keeping the world beautiful is just the same whether you are in the public park or in your own backyard. You will be able to think of dozens of ways in which every boy and girl is responsible for keeping the world a pleasant place to live in. This is the end of the chapter with a moral—*keep the world beautiful.*

BOOKS FOR FURTHER STUDY

Drawing and Painting

Bennett, J. F., *A Shady Hobby (Silhouettes)*. Bruce Publishing Company, 1944.

Bradshaw, Percy V., *I Wish I Could Draw*. Studio Publications, Inc., 1941.

Brown, Gregory, *How to Draw Trees*. Studio Publications, Inc., 1941.

Cuneo, T. T., *Tanks and How to Draw Them*. The Macmillan Company, 1942.

Doust, Len A., *A Manual on Drawing the Human Figure*. Bridgman Publishers, 1936.

Downer, Marion, *Be an Artist*. Lothrop, Lee and Shepard Company, 1941.

Guisti, George, *Drawing Figures*. Studio Publications, Inc., 1944.

Kruckman, Herbert L., *Of Course You Can Draw*. The Citadel Press, 1945.

Lawson, Philip A., *Practical Perspective Drawing*. McGraw-Hill Book Company, 1943.

Loomis, Andrew, *Figure Drawing for All It's Worth*. The Viking Press, 1943.

Pelikan, Alfred G., *Fun With Figure Drawing*. The Bruce Publishing Company, 1947.

Sheppard, Raymond, *How to Draw Birds*. Studio Publications, Inc., 1940.

Skeaping, John, *Animal Drawing*. Studio Publications, Inc., 1940.

———, *How to Draw Horses*. Studio Publications, Inc., 1941.

Thorne, Diana, *Drawing Dogs*. Studio Publications, Inc., 1940.

Vernam, Roger, *Drawing People for Fun*. McGraw-Hill Book Company, 1943.

Wood, Charles, *How to Draw Portraits*. Studio Publications, Inc., 1943.

Wootton, Frank, *How to Draw Planes*. Studio Publications, Inc., 1941.

Craftwork

Allen, Edith Louise, *Rugmaking Craft.* Chas. A. Bennett Co., Inc., 1945.

Bell, Enid, *Practical Wood-Carving Projects.* Harper and Brothers, 1940.

Bradley, Charles R., *Design in the Industrial Arts.* Chas. A. Bennett Co., Inc., 1946.

Coates, Helen, *Weaving for Amateurs.* Studio Publications, Inc., 1940.

Cox, Doris and Weisman, Barbara, *Creative Hands.* John Wiley and Sons, Inc., 1945.

Gaba, Lester, *Soap Carving.* Studio Publications, Inc., 1940.

Gallinger, Osma C., *The Joy of Weaving.* International Textbook Company, 1950.

Groneman, Chris H., *Applied Leathercraft.* Chas. A. Bennett Co., Inc., 1952.

Hallen, Julienne, *Folk Art Designs.* Home Crafts: New York, 1949.

Handicrafts for Children. Chas. A. Bennett Co., Inc., 1941.

Jenkins, R. Horace, *Practical Pottery.* Bruce Publishing Company, 1941.

Moore, Harris W., *Chip Carving.* Chas. A. Bennett Co., Inc., 1942.

Newkirk, Louis V. and Zutter, Lavada, *Crafts for Everyone.* International Textbook Company, 1950.

Powers, Margaret, *A Book of Little Crafts.* Chas. A. Bennett Co., Inc., 1942.

Pyle, Clifford, *Leathercraft as a Hobby.* Harper and Brothers, 1940.

Radtke, O. Arnold, *Kenne Cement Craft.* Bruce Publishing Company, 1943.

Sanger, Arthur and Lucille, *Cabochon Jewelry Making.* Chas. A. Bennett Co., Inc., 1950.

Shanklin, Margaret Eberhardt, *Use of Native Craft Materials.* Chas. A. Bennett Co., Inc., 1947.

Sprague, Curtis, *How to Make It.* Bridgman Publishers, 1941.

Design

Downer, Marion, *Discovering Design.* Lothrop, Lee, and Shepard Company, 1947.

Smith, Janet K., *Design: A Laboratory Manual.* Reinhold Publishing Corporation, 1950.

Reiss, Winold and Schweizer, Albert C., *You Can Design.* McGraw-Hill Book Company, 1939.

Lettering and Commercial Art

Bairnsfeather, Bruce, *Jeeps and Jests*. G. P. Putnam's Sons, 1943.

Biegeleisen, Jacob I., *The ABC of Lettering*. Harper and Brothers, 1940.

———, *Careers in Commercial Art*. E. P. Dutton and Company, 1944.

Brinkley, John, *Design for Printing*. Chas. A. Bennett Co., Inc., 1949.

Craven, Thomas, *Cartoon Cavalcade*. Simon and Schuster, 1943.

Eisenberg, James, *Commercial Art of Showcard Lettering*. D. Van Nostrand, Inc., 1945.

Ogg, Oscar, *An Alphabet Source Book*. Harper and Brothers, 1940.

Perry, Raymond W., *Blackboard Illustration*. Chas. A. Bennett Co., Inc., 1945.

Thompson, Tommy, *The ABC of Our Alphabet*. Studio Publications, Inc., 1942.

Cartoons and Caricatures

Epstein, Alvin, *How to Draw Animated Cartoons*. Greenberg Publisher, 1945.

Larias, Lawrence, *Careers in Cartooning*. Dodd, Mead, and Company, 1949.

Greene, Frank F., *How to Create Cartoons*. Harper and Brothers, 1941.

Sheridan, Martin, *Comics and Their Creators*. Watson-Guptil Publications, 1942.

Smith, Mitchell, *Art of Caricaturing*. Frederick J. Drake & Company, 1941.

Art Appreciation

Bartlet, F. G. and Crawford, C. C., *Art for All*. Harper and Brothers, 1942.

Caffin, Charles H., *How to Study Pictures*. D. Appleton-Century Company, 1941.

Chase, Alice Elizabeth, *Famous Paintings*. The Platt and Munk Company, Inc., 1951.

Christensen, Erwin O., *Popular Art in the United States*. Penquin Books, 1948.

Downer, Marion, *Paul Cezanne*. Lothrop, Lee and Shepard Company, 1951.

Hurlimann, Bettina, *Children's Portraits*. Thames and Hudson, 1950.

Kainz, C. Luise, and Riley, Olive T., *Exploring Art*. Harcourt, Brace and Company, 1947.

Lee, Kathryn D. and Burchwood, Katharine Tyler, *Art Then and Now*. Appleton-Century-Crofts, Inc., 1949.

Art in the Home

Austin, Ruth E., and Parvis, Jeanette O., *Furnishing Your Home*. Houghton Mifflin Company, 1952.

Brown, Effa, *Designs for Living*. Halycon House, 1942.

Gillies, Mary Davis, *Popular Home Decoration*. William H. Wise and Company, 1940.

———, *All About Modern Decorating*. Harper and Brothers, 1948.

Ketcham, Howard, *How to Use Color and Decorating Designs*. Greystone Press, 1949.

Lewis, Ethel, *Decorating the Home*. The Macmillan Company, 1942.

Merivale, Margaret, *Furnishing the Small Home*. Studio Publications, Inc., 1940.

Ornstein, J. A., *Paintbrush Fun for Home Decoration*. Greenberg Publisher, 1944.

Robertson, Florence Bell, *Planting Design*. McGraw-Hill Book Company, 1940.

Trilling, Mabel B., and Williams, Florence, *Art in Home and Dress*. J. B. Lippincott Company, 1942.

Wright, Mary and Russell, *Guide to Easier Living*. Simon and Schuster, 1951.

INDEX